ESCAPE FROM LONELINESS

By
PAUL TOURNIER

Escape from Loneliness

Translated by
JOHN S. GILMOUR

THE WESTMINSTER PRESS

Philadelphia

LIBRARY OF CONGRESS CATALOG CARD No. 61–14599

To my friends

THEO SPOERRI AND PHILIPPE MOTTU,
*a mark of affection and admiration for their
effort in restoring the sense of community
and fellowship in our Helvetia*

Contents

Translator's Note

Dr. Tournier is always refreshing. If the present translation has preserved much of his clarity of expression, as well as a certain artful style, then the translator's labors have been more than adequately rewarding.

It was recently my privilege to spend thirteen months in specialized clinical studies in Louisville, Kentucky. There, I became aware of the vast amount of pioneering in the relationship of theology and psychology that is going on in America. Nevertheless, as a bilingual Canadian who has discovered some of the wealth of scholarship and research in French-speaking Europe, it has seemed to me that we North Americans unnecessarily miss the contribution of European counterparts. This is because we are limited, in our reading, to the English language. I hope that the present volume may contribute to an ever-increasing exchange of knowledge and experience between America and Europe.

JOHN S. GILMOUR

Montreal, Canada
June, 1961

These lines are being jotted down on my way back to Europe from a two-month tour of the United States. My Philadelphia publisher has asked me to add a personal word for my American readers. To do so is a pleasure. It is my opportunity to say how much we are impressed, both Mrs. Tournier and myself, by the warm welcome given us in this land, and to express our gratitude to all those who showed us so much kindness, especially Prof. John B. Graham, of the University of North Carolina, who organized our trip.

It was to my great surprise that my book, *The Meaning of Persons*, provoked such interest in the United States. In this first book published in English (by Harper & Brothers), I contrasted our " personage " or social mask, with our " person," that is, our intimate and deeper being. Well, to Europeans such as we, Americans seem so much more spontaneous and sincere. They have nothing of our reserve. They give themselves wholeheartedly and without reserve, with zest and friendliness. This impression of Americans was confirmed over and over again for me throughout our tour along the East Coast, in the Chicago area, and out along the Pacific. Right as soon as we meet them, Americans offer their friendship, no strings attached.

I have often spoken of this here. I have remarked that Europeans seem to me more like " personages," role players, enslaved to their traditions and social conventions — distant. My

9

American colleagues have replied that this warm and open welcome that we find in their midst is also, to a certain extent, a socially imposed pattern, a role or "personage," a façade behind which they may well hide their intimate selves, just as Europeans do behind their apparent coldness.

The problem of fellowship, or "community," which is the subject matter of this present book, may well lead to similar conclusions. I wrote the book because the emotional isolation of modern men had deeply impressed me. I had discovered this loneliness through my day-to-day counseling practice in Europe. In America, on the other hand, the importance given to social life literally hits you in the eyes. Americans love to be in groups. The tendency toward withdrawal that is so marked in Europe seems to be almost unknown in this land. Their need of togetherness, their pleasure in social life, their sometimes all-too-childlike spontaneity, their uninhibited laughter that breaks forth at a word and that seems to us more artless than funny — all this social pleasure so universally in evidence stands in stark contrast with the heavy weariness that characterizes so often our European masses.

Yet, in spite of all this, do they experience true fellowship any more than we in Europe? Only Americans will be able to judge. I do not in the least want to cast any doubt. Their taste for social friendship strikes me as fresh, artless, authentic. However, the gregarious instinct may not suffice in order to achieve fellowship. It may well be that the deeper experience of fellowship has as one of its necessary conditions that we first achieve a creative solitude. All living phenomena obey laws of complementary alternation, such as the pulsations of the heart and the succession of seasons. Doubtless, this is equally true of social life and fellowship. Its full value is reserved for those who at other times can do without it, and can live an autonomous and personal life.

It is this kind of questioning that adds so much interest to the dialogue between North Americans and Europeans, this dialogue which I enjoyed so much while traveling through

America, speaking to so many perceptive listeners, and listening to them in turn, as we considered our world's needs and sought together how we would better answer them. I hope that this book may contribute to that answer by sharing with Americans something of the experience of a European.

PAUL TOURNIER

Grand Forks, North Dakota
May, 1961

I

Loneliness

I

". . . and so, we bid you a very pleasant good night! "

Often she used to turn on the radio in the evening, just as the program ended, in order to hear these few words, in order to hear a human voice wish her good night. Yet, she worked as a secretary of an international welfare organization. Her boss, a fine man, had dedicated his whole life to the battle against a social scourge. Many visitors from every country came to see him, but in the office they spoke only business. Never was there a word addressed to her as a person. Who she was, how she, a foreigner, had come to Geneva after many ups and downs, the sorrows that still deeply troubled her — nobody cared about these things. Her work was appreciated, and she received every courtesy, but to all intents and purposes she remained alone.

She lived in one of those great modern buildings, with countless one-room flats, where the neighbors' noises come from every floor. She knew none of those neighbors with whom she rubbed shoulders in the elevator daily, and they did not know her. She had no intimate friends. Her room was even in the same building where she worked. She rarely went out for any reason except for the odd hurried shopping trip. Before falling asleep, she would switch on the radio, ". . . and so, we bid you a very pleasant good night! " It was a human voice, speaking *to her.*

One morning, her boss came into the office with a strange look on his face. "From now on," he said, "I would like God to be the real boss here, and for all of us to accept his leadership and authority. No welfare work can be effective unless men come to God and seek his spirit, not only in their churches, but in their homes, in their offices, and in their factories."

He had met an Anglican bishop, who was on the way through Geneva from the Far East. He had spoken for a long time with the bishop, and had come to realize that only a living faith was the real answer to man's great suffering. Through the many years of his service, he had come to see the extent of such suffering.

It brought a complete upheaval in his secretary's life. She entered into a whole new relationship with her boss, no longer a purely business relationship, but a human one. He unburdened his soul to her, and spoke to her as a person. What he told her awakened in her a multitude of questions of which she had never spoken to anyone. Soon she too was revived to faith. She unburdened herself, in turn. She made countless new friends. It was then that my wife and I met this young woman. We discovered how inexpressibly lonely her life had been up until then, and of which no one would have been aware had it not been for the Anglican bishop's visit in Geneva.

How many men and women around about us there are, with whom we rub shoulders daily, living in the same kind of secret loneliness. The doctor, a sort of confessor, knows it better than anyone else. Often at the close of an interview I have heard the client tell me, "Without realizing it, I have been looking for someone for many years, someone to whom I could say just what I've told you now, someone whom I could trust without reservation and without any fear of being condemned."

One day, one of my colleagues and friends said to me: "I believe that if there are so many housemaids who come to consult us, it is not because they are sicker than others; it is because they hunger for human fellowship. In the doctor's office they are persons just as much as their bosses, and no longer just hired help who count only for the job they do."

Every doctor knows what the terrible loneliness of modern man is. " People," writes Dr. Tina Keller, " have become more and more isolated." I could take hundreds of examples from my daily practice. A young woman, a complete stranger to me, came and asked me for a hospital admittance form. Another doctor had made a recommendation that she be operated on for chronic appendicitis as soon as she could arrange for it. There was nothing unusual about this consultation! We spoke for a moment, and then I learned that this woman, at logger-heads with her own family, had left her husband a few months after the wedding to follow another lover who now had walked out on her. She was living alone, without relatives or friends, without a job, not daring to go back to her home town for fear of meeting her husband again.

Here is another whose troubles were only the symptoms of her mental distress. She had given her life to care for her mother, whom she tenderly loved, and who was her only friend. They had lived for each other for years. Her mother had re-cently died. She had worked for a long time in her brother's shop, but since he had married, she was made to feel that she should look for other employment. There, she no longer had anyone close to her. She was alone.

How many others there are who have been isolated by chronic sickness or infirmity! At first, their friends rally to them somewhat; later on they gradually drop off, so that the doctor becomes their sole tie with the world.

Then there are those placed in some hospital or asylum be-cause their care was too much of a drag upon their families. There, in overcrowded wards, they feel that they are but num-bers, case histories, to the nurse or medical staff making their rounds.

There are those too who have a family, but who for some reason that they do not understand, have come to feel alienated from them, and now, alone, lead a discouraging life with only a cat as their friend.

The family will tell you that the mother has no one to blame but herself, that she had always been difficult to get along with, that she'd always been unsociable, hypersensitive, and withdrawn. If you question them further about their childhood, you will understand their reasons more clearly.

Children are sensitive, sometimes keenly so. Read Weatherhead's fine chapter on this subject. "Teasing a child," he writes, "only forces him into a desperate loneliness." At derision from his brothers, sisters, or as is often the case, from his parents, he withdraws into himself. One of my clients who stuttered somewhat, had, because of the teacher, been exposed for a whole year to the ridicule of her class. The result can be surmised. Another told me, "I've never been able to trust anyone ever since, as a little child, my best friend told a secret that I had shared with him."

The mother of one of my patients used to amuse herself in the evening by terrorizing her child with a hideous little doll dressed up as the devil.

There are yet many other wounds, even deeper. A certain father, for example, of whom Weatherhead speaks, who in his wounded pride and solicitude for his child would say to him: "I wonder what you'll ever do in life. You can't do anything much. Who will ever hire you on?" The child sobs, "No one likes me," and soon, "O God, why did you let me be born?"

"My mother is very sentimental," another lonely soul told me. "When I was small she always wanted affection from me, and that made me withdraw from her. As for my father, his work was his life. He never showed any interest in me."

Here is another such sensitive person, victim of an extreme timidity, who kicks himself for not being able to marry simply because he is unable to approach a girl, and who is obsessed by it, and thus is further isolated and driven to greater anxiety. His childhood was lived in total emotional isolation. His vulgar and brutal father, a livestock buyer, terrified him, and his mother sought compensation in him for her affection needs, which only repulsed the child further.

A certain teacher had her young pupils write about their fathers. She discovered real anguish in many of them; their fathers seemed to them distant and withdrawn. They felt their fathers to be engrossed in their own affairs, which mystery the children vainly tried to understand. They wondered what they could do to help their fathers. Doubtless the latter would say, as so many have said to me, " I never speak of my troubles at home so as not to upset the family." They fail to see that every member of the family senses the troubles, and would be less troubled if they could bear them with the father. The fathers are making their families a training ground for solitude.

Another withdrawn child has been crushed by the authoritarian discipline of his father who is unconsciously getting vengeance for the authority from which he suffered in his childhood.

What throws the child most often into emotional isolation is conflict between the parents, disputes and violence which he witnesses, and which terrify him. Some have wished to mediate between the parents and the blows fell on them. Now they lock themselves up in their room when the storms break out.

The parents, carried away by the passion of the argument and blinded by their feelings, do not realize how deeply their child is torn apart inwardly. Instinctively he wants to keep his parents united, to embrace them in the same love, but he feels powerless in the face of their conflict. Often he is in turn made the witness for his father, or for his mother, and the confidant for their recriminations against each other. While his parents keep turning over their resentments in their hearts, the child hides himself under the bedcovers every evening and cries in secret, sometimes for years. When these parents divorce, they tell us quite sincerely that it is for their child's sake so that he will no longer be under the bad influence of the other partner.

A teacher told me that one day, while straightening out the desk for a small pupil whose hypersensitivity worried her, she found a photo at the bottom. It was of the mother who had left home. The child blushed and said confusedly, " Excuse me, ma'am, but it's the only place I can put her because I dare not take her home."

If we stop to think that Switzerland has 50,000 children of divorced parents, then we can understand how much the spirit of our times tends toward isolation — isolation and mistrust. (Translator's note: In America, the number of such children of divorce is *proportionately* almost three times that of Switzerland. That is, there are over 4,000,000 children of divorced parents here!) The teacher of one such child of divorced parents pointed out to me that he had nothing to do with his classmates. Another day, the boy told me, with a look on his face that betrayed his suffering, " I distrust everybody."

Since a child is sensitive, and knows nothing yet about life, the father has only to raise his voice a little in order to upset him. He reacts to a simple discussion, which the parents never think twice about, as if it were a serious conflict.

Terrifying memories of parental fights are the most recurring factor that we find in the histories of the anxious and withdrawn who come to consult us. It takes love, tact, and much time in order to help them break down walls behind which they have imprisoned themselves. After several months' interviews, one of them wrote me, " I am shocked at my thought: why not adopt a positive attitude toward life instead of being like a hedgehog and curling up at the smallest provocation? "

The children are at stake in any parental conflict. They are, in turn, spoiled and threatened, praised and disparaged, exposed to all the contradictions and about turns brought on by the ups and downs of the tragic conflict. One moment understanding nothing, a moment later they see all too clearly what their parents are about. When one of them wants to have the children visit the grandparents, or decides to board them out, the other refuses. Each parent is convinced that he or she is inspired by the child's welfare solely. This is simply rationalizing — that is, the mind's provision of good reasons for what is dictated by passion. The child, with his sensitive intuition, senses this, knows that he really doesn't count in spite of the show of affection showered on him, sometimes even in excess.

Many such children have given me the memoirs of their childhood to read, written in order to unburden their heart. They do not dare publish them for fear of shaming their family. If only parents in conflict could read such poignant pages, their eyes might be opened to the unknown sufferings they are sowing for all of life in the soul of their child.

The same is true of many couples who never come to divorce, and who often sincerely believe that they have kept the conflict unknown to the children. But children are never fooled by the lie. They see through the parents' unconscious, yes, even sincere, lies. This has repercussions upon the relationships between the children, either by compensatory affection fixations, or by terrible hostility between those on the mother's side and those on the father's, hostility which the children prolong long after they've forgotten its cause.

These children guard all through life a sort of savior complex, a sentimental tenderness for all who seem to be victims of injustice, but have neither the self-discipline nor the necessary authority to come to their aid effectively.

The bizarre behavior, distant and yet pitiable, to which the wounds of their childhood experience push them only further contributes to isolate them in life. High-strung people are not generally liked. Dr. Dubois compares them to " the stragglers in the Army corps. They are a little less severely treated . . . but they are not liked. They are quickly reproached to their face with being lazy, fakers, and weaklings. No one knows whether to believe their ills and put them in the infirmary, or to be rough with them and send them to work."

In life, more often than not, they get rough treatment. Hence they withdraw increasingly into themselves.

II

It would be wrong to think that this feeling of loneliness strikes only the nervous and the withdrawn. That would be attributing it to occasional personal incidents, when it is widespread and is the result of the spirit of our age.

Formerly, man was controlled by social class: the family, the indissolubility of the marital bonds plus the filial respect imposed by tradition, the intimacy reigning in the craftsman's shop, the homogeneity of the trade guild, the cohesiveness of the city, and especially the community of faith and of moral, spiritual, and social ideas brought about by the church — all these gave a framework to individual life. I do not pretend that man was any better, that he was, for example, in his heart any more faithful to his wife because public opinion did not allow him divorce! But a community of ideas bound him to the society of which he was a part. Today, on the other hand, he is lost in the anonymity of the large city and of big business. He is tossed to and fro by the most contradictory ideologies and dazzled by a popularized science that brings him more illusions than knowledge. Left alone to make the most perilous of intellectual experiments — that of developing his own philosophy of life, he lacks the necessary cultural means. He is the victim of a confusion never before known in his history, and he feels himself to be alone. Speak to him of the family, and he will answer "outworn traditions." Speak to him of the native land, and you will get "exploitation of the people."

Add to that the mix-up of peoples brought about by economic evolution. Here is a German-Swiss couple having lived in a small town of French Switzerland for many years; they don't mix with anyone, they haven't made a single friend, they haven't even learned French.

Nor let us forget all those modest families in our suburbs, changing neighborhoods every other year without ever taking root.

There are jovial and social people who can attract others about them and tell endless stories but who have as much difficulty in talking freely of what really is close to their hearts as the most withdrawn individual.

Here is a teacher for whom her class is but an anonymous and hostile group. She finds personal relationships neither there nor among her fellow teachers, each jealous of his independence. In the solitude of her small room, she would at least like to work, to write, but finds herself paralyzed by an undefinable uneasiness, an inner torment.

Here is a young woman who has taken on important social responsibilities abroad. She had come home to visit her aged mother. Both of them cherished in their innermost hearts a deep affection for one another, but felt powerless to express it. Both told me of their desire to break the ice, to find each other by way of the heart, and of their despair at not having come to that place. The girl's emancipation had opened her to an intellectual world which her mother was unable to understand; yet her inner enrichment could not console her for the mental loneliness into which this emancipation had plunged her.

Here is a woman of high ideals and wide experience whose ideas were discussed with a great deal of interest, and who had numerous admirers, but who desired to give the world something else besides ideas to discuss. She would have liked to accomplish a personal work, to win hearts and to exert upon them a profound influence. She did not know how to go about it. The very esteem which surrounded her isolated her.

Here is a university professor whose works are authorities and who, behind the imposing front of his intellectual career, hides a desperate thirst for fellowship which he finds neither with his wife, his children, nor his colleagues.

Here is a professor of psychology, quite stiff in his family life, incapable of understanding his wife or of gaining the attention of his children.

Here is a social nurse who chose her vocation because of the ideal of giving herself for others. She is appreciated for her work, overloaded with jobs. But after a few years a feeling of having been deceived comes over her; her work appears to her so shallow; she runs from one " case " to another without ever having time to get to know anyone. She has to meet people on the " outside," inquire into their life histories without being able to understand them from the inside, without discovering the impenetrable recess of their souls. With her superiors and her colleagues, she must always talk shop. There's never any time for becoming intimate or for unburdening herself. In the midst of a fruitful social career, she feels alone.

Here is a man in politics, carried away by the fray of public life. He has the appearance of a leader, but the hard demands of his career have completely isolated him from his family. He has become a stranger to them. His political enemies have become for him only forces to fight against. His own partisans are only pawns on the political chessboard. He is made use of, he is praised, or he is fought, but no one is interested in *him*, or in his inner, gnawing anxieties.

Thus modern man's loneliness is not the mark of those defeated in life, the sensitive, or the nervous only, but equally of the leaders, of the elite.

We have so effectively preached a "sincerity" in personal convictions that the most devoted people hold themselves back from the crowd and no longer find any community with which they can fully associate themselves. There is always a doctrinal or practical matter to which they cannot sincerely subscribe. They are repulsed by all mass movements and by everything that might be propaganda, and leave these in the hands of shallower minds. This is the great divorce between the elite and the people.

This tragic isolation of the elite is present most acutely in the church, especially in the Protestant Church. Among religious people there are many of a deep spirituality who could and should help the world to awaken to its soul and to put an end to its tremendous moral confusion. However, they move in a world of their own, speak a language of their own, and in their passion for sincerity part company with each other along a thousand different ways.

I have rarely felt the modern man's isolation more grippingly than in a certain deaconess or a certain pastor. Carried away in the activism rampant in the church, the latter holds meeting upon meeting, always preaching, even in personal conversation, with a program so burdened that he no longer finds time for meditation, never opening his Bible except to find subjects for his sermons. It no longer nourishes him personally. One such pastor, after several talks with me, said abruptly, " I'm always praying as a pastor, but for a long time now I've never prayed simply as a man."

Among colleagues, they discuss theology, church affairs, and sometimes even pastoral care, but they practice no mutual pastoral care. They struggle alone with their inextricable family problems, with their temptations, with the guilt of their secret faults, never daring to unburden themselves to their colleagues or to their parishioners because they are afraid of being condemned or of causing a scandal. I have known one pastor who used to confess to a priest in order to find inner peace. Even when doubt steals into their heart, they still have to preach, unless they dare to seek out a psychotherapeutic clinic in order once again to find themselves and to rebuild their faith, shattered by deceptions, disobediences, and loneliness.

It is the church alone, nevertheless, which can answer the world of today's tremendous thirst for community. Christ sent his disciples two by two. The great body of the early Christians, according to the Bible, "were of one heart and soul"; "they had all things in common" (Acts 4:32; 2:44). Instead of demonstrating the way to fellowship to the world today, the church seems to embody the triumph of individualism. The faithful sit side by side without even knowing each other; the elders gather in a little parliament with its parties and formalities; the pastors do their work without reference to one another.

Among the great denominations, the rivalry, though happily less violent than formerly, still reminds us of the hostility that separates the nations of the world. Each denounces the errors of the other, instead of admitting its own. "The emphasis should not be put upon what separates us," writes a medical doctor, "but upon what unites us, Jesus Christ our one Lord."

This reminds me of an incident in the Army; this division of the churches provides ample subject matter for the skeptics. In the officers' mess, an ordinary conversation turned suddenly to the religious sphere, and the colonel began satirizing Catholic ritual. In order to tease another officer known for his religious convictions, he challenged him, " What do we Protestants have in common with the Catholics? " The latter, taking up the challenge in a clear voice that imposed respect, answered, " Just one small detail, Colonel, our Lord Jesus Christ! "

Within Protestantism, how many fights among diverse denominations and theological schools of thought where human pride flourishes! This was not the Reformers' purpose. A philosopher as ' neutral ' as Bréhier can write: " The Reformation's spirit of free inquiry is tailor-made for the gradual suppression, by means of independent criticism, of all that Bossuet called ' particular opinions ' and ' variations.' It thus became a means of arriving at ' catholicity,' even though by a route other than authority."

Here is a sick woman, right in the crisis of mental derangement, to whom I was called. A few months later we were able to converse rationally. I learned that for a long time she had been under the pressure of two sects simultaneously; each one in turn claiming to possess all the truth and that everything of the other was of the devil. She did not have the theological development necessary to maintain a certain critical attitude and her soul was literally torn in two to the point of insanity. This erupted when another convert tried to force her into a mystical experience, and then when that failed, told her that she was demon-possessed.

The state church criticizes the sects and their theological errors, but fails to see that if the people turn to them it is because they are homesick for a close fellowship, which their church has not known how to provide.

Without even taking into account sectarian excesses, we can see the individualistic deviation within Protestantism when we consider one of its deepest and most admirable thinkers, Kierkegaard, who puts " the soul in the presence of God, absolutely alone."

The hermit in his hut can be in communion with men whereas the believer in church, anxious to be sincere, can be spiritually alone. Yet, in the words of one of my patients, spoken the other day, "there are two things you cannot do alone: marry, and be a Christian."

I have had to care for many people spiritually uprooted, and I have been able to weigh their sufferings. They are victims of this modern call to an exaggerated sincerity which ignores the need for spiritual fellowship. One such uprooted woman, long a fervent Catholic, had become friends with one of these free-thinkers who had troubled her and had aroused in her criticism of her church's priest. This patient had not taken Communion for a long time because she had doubts about confession to this particular priest. Her uprooting was so unmistakably one of the factors in her psychic troubles that I ended up by saying, " The first condition of your healing is the renewal within you of the flow of grace! " I wrote to a very understanding priest, from whom she could receive her Easter Communion.

I think of various women of simple faith, married to intel-lectuals, doctors, learned men — who have completely shaken them in the faith they had received, without having helped them to rebuild a personal religious life. One day the husband is frightened to see the psychological disaster brought about by him in his wife and for which he can offer no answer because he does not understand the religious problem himself.

One woman, a soul eminently sensitive and deep, born a Catholic, was converted to Protestantism under influences which naturally I would not criticize. For her it was from an inner maturity and a sincere will to obey the leading of the Spirit, all of which bore spiritual fruit. Nevertheless, this change from one religion to another is a trial, for one no longer belongs completely to either, especially if he is more or less left to fend for himself in his new church. I must say that for this woman, the trial never ended in complete victory, shown by certain anxiety doubts, a continuing self-degrading attitude, and an obsessive return to the question of her salvation.

Naturally, the same is true of a certain Protestant who became Catholic in order to find the liturgical and authoritarian support of which he felt the need, but in whom I see the same type of inner disturbance. The stamp of condemnatory criticisms of Catholicism received in his childhood has made it impossible for him to be wholeheartedly absorbed therein, despite his religious zeal in the attempt.

There are so many others, tossed about by all the conflicting currents of thought unleashed in the modern world, who never succeed in becoming rooted, who float, so to speak, between two churches or between atheism and faith, or who go successively from one group to another, always with zeal but never able to commit themselves for good.

This is a very touchy matter to mention, and I do so with reverence. For the most part, it is a question of noble souls sincerely desiring to obey God and loyally seeking through these detours the deep spiritual experience for which they long. I never stop them in their quest, for it is possible for them to find what they are looking for. However, generally their spiritual life bears little fruit, always stumbling against certain realities which they cannot sincerely accept in any church. Their very spirituality ends up in isolating them rather than in bringing them together with others. There are certain blessings found only in fellowship and in total surrender to one's church.

III

Such is the loneliness of man discovered by the doctor daily in his office. He has a rather individual ministry, fulfilled in face-to-face relationships. He does not deal with society as such. However, he must bring his message in view of the world's great tragic situation. As he enters daily into the lives of so many families torn by strife, he comes to see why peace is impossible among the nations and the social classes. He sees that men's loneliness is linked with fear. Men fear one another, fear to be crushed in life, fear to be misunderstood. The doctor knows that fear is a universal and natural feeling, though everyone seeks to hide it. " Until the age of reason," writes Dr. Forel, " the child, like the animal, fears noise, silence, night, wind, thunder, everything that is not mother or family." He adds, " Whether it is the famous ' class warfare,' strikes, salary movements, world, local, or colonial wars, the deep-down motive remains the same: man seeks to strengthen his security, seeks to assuage his original anguish."

Thus, fear breeds loneliness and conflict; loneliness and conflict breed fear. To heal the world, we must give men an answer to fear and restore among them the sense of community.

The doctor hears, as well, secrets about social life. He can envisage this all-pervading competition which throws the very men who should be working together against one another, in spite of all their good will. He knows how suspicious feelings poison office life; because a certain employee is in good with the boss, she can irritate her fellows and sow unfairness and division. He understands the jealousies that separate the heads of rival firms just as much as two workmen in the same factory, two artists, two scholars, or two deaconesses.

It is especially in the family conflicts, daily brought to him, that the doctor is able to judge the extent to which the feeling of togetherness is lost. He discovers there, point by point, everything that is characteristic of the terrible struggles between nations. " The same warfare that unfolds on world-wide scale has its effect in the family, and in the individual soul," writes Dr. Tina Keller.

In a family conflict, each partner always has legitimate complaints to make; in the name of justice and moral principle he states his case. Each one has his " bureau of propaganda " and presents his side quite sincerely in such a way as to justify himself unquestionably. There are preventive provocations, suspicions regarding any conciliatory move by the other, or a war of nerves which compels one partner to do the very thing needed to aggravate the conflict.

I dedicate a great deal of my activity trying to reconcile marital partners, but I must admit the difficult and tiring task it is.

Each tries to put me in his camp. He very quickly suspects that I am allied with the other, if I try to remain objective as well as understanding and charitable toward him.

Most tragic of all are the numerous couples who, though each of them has a sincere good will and strong desire to rediscover their oneness, never achieve this. Their best-intentioned words and acts produce the opposite effect, as if by diabolical fate. Often each partner trusts me completely, and I am able to have true spiritual fellowship with each. Yet they remain strangers to each other, unable either to open up to — or to understand — each other, both of them bitterly deceived at not feeling understood.

At such times I feel that there are powerful negative powers, emanating from the spirit of our age and beyond the scope of the individual, which are blocking the most loyal efforts exerted to re-create the feeling of togetherness. Then it is that I can sense what obstacles that statesmen must face in bringing together nations and social classes. The pressure of public opinion is everywhere toward division, competition, opposition. In family conflicts I often feel that I'm alone in going against an all-powerful current. Pity by relatives and friends fans the flames. They whisper in each partner's ear, "If I were you, I'd have left him long ago; I'd never tolerate such behavior in my husband; your patience has become sinful collusion with evil against what is right!"

Sometimes one of the partners comes to tell me in a triumphant tone of voice that a certain outstanding person whom he has consulted has agreed with him that divorce is the only solution.

We realize therefore that individual efforts cannot suffice unless supported by a radical reform in popular attitudes. The whole philosophy of our age produces in modern men an independent, possessive, and vengeful spirit that sets them against one another. It is supposed to lead them to happiness; the result is the accumulation of suffering in discord and loneliness.

Dr. Dubois, of Bern, wrote that the doctor's task was noth-

ing less than "a complete change of attitude in the patient."
One does not need to be a doctor to realize that the whole
world is sick, and that healing depends upon such a basic reform in our attitudes. It is toward this goal that this book is
dedicated in the hope that it may help and encourage the large
number of men who have undertaken this task in various
spheres — political, educational, social, and economic.

II

The Parliamentary Spirit

I

I have always admired those champion chess players who may carry on as many as thirty games simultaneously against as many able competitors. This is the kind of picture that each man's relationship to his surrounding world gives us today. His ambition is to succeed in life. He sees life as one big tournament, with success as the winner's prize. His professional success, his acquired social prestige, his honors in university or in sports, his success in love, the good reputation of his family, the triumph of his party, of his country, or of his ideas, plus a thousand other concerns — these represent so many simultaneous games that he carries on right from youth to old age.

His family, his friends, his pupils, his bosses or his employees, are so many chessmen moving about on his chessboard, who through their successes and failures, glories and shames, bear directly upon his strategic position. The look of admiration that his wife receives at the social or that his daughter receives while playing tennis, the congratulations he receives when his son receives his doctorate, the successful publication of his book, the envy that his automobile arouses, a word of tenderness from his wife — all these are so many points to be marked down in his favor. But discredit heaped upon him for failure, an insult or an injustice done to a friend or relative, or to his party, are so many blows that jeopardize his tournament.

The tournament is rough! Each man carefully plays his game, seeking to better his position by skillful moves or to recuperate from a bad move, losing the fewest chessmen possible. Each success makes the game easier; each loss makes it more arduous. How much worrying there is of the what-might-happen, and how much daydreaming of miraculous recoveries!

Thus every home, shop, classroom, office, or conference is a field of combat where each one tries his luck. Alliances are made, coalitions are combated, propaganda is carefully devised. Thus two families, to foster a marriage of their children each of whom flatters the other family, are both misled as to the other's financial situation by its lavish spending.

I believe that Darwin's hypothesis of the survival of the fittest as a factor in evolution has played a decisive role in forming our modern attitudes. In presenting nature as the theater of a universal struggle of beings, all fighting against one another so as not to be choked out, this hypothesis has suggested that life could be only competition, never co-operation. It has contributed greatly both to the widely accepted doctrine of class struggle and to economic liberalism, which held that the welfare of all would result from universal competition.

Lecomte du Noüy has said (in *L'avenir de l'Esprit*) that modern science differs from Darwin's conception by declaring that the changes that appear in each species throughout the geological eras " do not confer any immediate advantage to the animals thus furnished." As a matter of fact, nature presents to us the most impressive picture of universal co-operation. The chemical cycles, all the symbioses, the interdependence of vegetative and animal life, of the organs of a body, of the various species, and of all the functions and cells of an organism — all this bespeaks community and solidarity.

Hence it is that modern man, misled by nineteenth-century science and philosophy, can conceive of society only as a vast network of battles, tests of strength, and competition between rival powers.

This could be called the parliamentary spirit. Here is a family much like a miniature parliament. The parents take sides in every matter, like two parties in the legislature. If the father is stern, the mother secretly spoils the children. If he is generous, she tightens the purse strings. If she is religious, he feigns no belief at all. The children in turn choose sides. Parties are formed and a balance is established between them. They make demands on each other and compromise by one side's giving its assent on a given matter in exchange for personal advantages. The one in power makes the big decisions, whereas the opposition leader denounces his errors. Each exaggerates his rights in order to gain at least something. The family is no longer a unit, but a congress where representatives of different viewpoints meet one another, bound together by a legal contract and certain common interests. "The degradation of spiritual life," writes Elisabeth Huguenin in *Mission de la femme*, "has brought with it the degradation of relationships between the sexes. Where there ought to be a mutual strengthening, our age calls for the organization and compartmentalization of human activity; instead of the mystery of love, debate is called for; instead of a life of communion, each partner lives a separate life."

In this parliamentary spirit, family members meet one another on the outside, so to speak, just like congressmen. They never make contact with the other person deep down inside, but only with his outward role, his system of thought, his leanings or his demands. In this parliamentary game, with its subtle procedure, they can estimate very precisely the strength they have to deal with in the other members and the reactions they will have to maneuver, but they do not know the person himself, in his inner, complex being. "My husband," one of my clients told me, " seems like a mysterious island that I'm always encircling without ever finding a place to land."

Here is a mother who has always lined up with her daughters against her husband. They were more or less her personal property. Now she has lost one of them, and instead of this bringing her closer to her husband, it has left her more alone than ever, so much so that she has gone into a depression.

Parliamentary deputies are careful not to mention their party's inner dissensions to deputies of the other party, lest the latter use such knowledge as a weapon against them. Similarly, in the family it seems that one would jeopardize the whole balance of power if he were to admit to being wrong in a matter, if he were to reveal his inner conflicts or his moral failings. Yet, just such an admission would serve to remake the family into a community, " a person-to-person relationship."

Here is a young woman who speaks to me with complete trust about her doubts and her shattered hopes. She tells me also about her mother, from whom she feels so distant. When I ask her if she doesn't think she would get through to her mother's heart by telling her what she has just confided in me, her answer is, " I could never do that; I'm afraid she'd use it to dominate me even more."

Thus, each one hides his most personal concerns behind the false front of title, position, reputation, or doctrine. We debate, correct others, or criticize in order to avoid the questions we are asking of ourselves. Philippe Mottu writes that it is " the irresponsible 'you ought to' which changes a sound idea into useless chatter."

Hence social formalism, the middle-class front wherein everyone hides his weakness and failings behind rules, propriety, authority. I will dwell again upon the psychological catastrophe to which this leads. A man is at the top of society, covered with honors and university degrees, entrusted with important tasks in the church and in the government. But his son sees his father every day at home in an altogether different light — impulsive, violent, unfair. The father manages to evade his son's questions by treating him as impertinent, by remaining upon his pedestal of paternal and social authority. The very contrast between the brilliant social personage and the mean person he really is scars the simple child's soul and plunges him into neurosis.

Equally formalist, too, is the " do-gooder," whose charitable activities give a fine humanitarian appearance, but wherein the poor find only an unknowable machine that checks every impulse of the heart by rules.

When I worked in Vienna for the International Red Cross after the First War, I was in close contact with all the foreign societies helping the starving children. Some of them were most impressive and well-organized, feeding more than half a million children daily. However, their trucks went throughout the city as unnoticed as those of the government. On the other hand, the little Quaker Fords were cheered wherever they went, by a people who appreciated the joyful charity of those young people who visited two by two in the homes, talking to each person, finding out the needs, and returning with specially made up packages.

Often I have heard a patient tell me that he has been disappointed in his doctor, who yet had taken good care of him, "because he didn't take me seriously." The patient means that the doctor wasn't interested in detail, in particular problems that meant a great deal to his patient. "The patient," writes Dr. Dubois, "must be much more than just an interesting case; he must become your friend."

It is this fear of touching upon the personal which causes the overorganization of social and administrative activity. In order to avoid telling an applicant that we do not wish to admit him to a college, we quickly draw up a regulation that bars his entry by establishing an age limit. In order to avoid speaking as man to man to an employee about an error he has committed, a general order is drawn up and quite impersonally delivered to each man. And the regulations multiply. They completely dominate life in the office or the plant where there are no means of communication other than notices. Employees can work all their lives alongside one another without ever coming to know one another personally. Sometimes it is only at their colleague's funeral that they discover how many concerns they had in common with him. A certain employee never gets the impression that his personal life is of any interest to his superior. A candidate for a position is never asked concerning his ideals, his sense of vocation, his philosophy of life — all of which imply a value judgment. Rather, he is asked about his qualifications and his degrees, and if his age fits in with the retirement plan. Once when I hired a secretary of whom my wife had learned that she had the necessary moral qualities for effective teamwork, she immediately told me, in an anxious tone of voice, " But I don't have any degree! "

Thus is our life completely regulated. Each has his little trade-mark giving him the right to his little place in society. But it is a place, a function, a seat such as that of a congressman, and the man himself remains alone, without a personal relationship. The smallest amateur sports club or women's sewing circle devotes endless meetings to the drawing up and subsequent ceaseless amending of a constitution and, by a subtle procedure, creates posts of honor even to the point of having a vice-secretary.

Science itself depersonalizes man, as William James has remarked. The biologist, Lecomte du Noüy, of Pasteur Institute, has written (in *Le temps et la vie*) a few brilliant pages on this subject. He says: " The romance of discovery is a personal and thrilling adventure for the scientist. However, when he writes up his dissertation, the conventions of custom oblige him to eliminate the 'individual factor,' the 'personal coefficient,' and to repress everything that stirred up his heart in that great adventure behind the impersonal presentation of an exposé which cannot touch the heart of the reader."

Right from school the child is exposed to this formal type of teaching, which aims at preparing him for an intellectual and social function more than it aims at developing his person. As early as the Renaissance, Petrus Ramus denounced this formalism of the school that Aristotle bequeathed to us. If that master of the ancient world was a true father and personal friend for the disciples who shared his life, the modern school is anonymous when for the most part the teacher shares nothing of that which gives his life real taste, his pupils being little more than numbers.

I was in my teens when I was first instructed by the teacher who influenced me most. He was an old Hellenist who used to invite me to his home, alone, almost every month. This continued over several years, even after I had long ceased to be his pupil. He talked about his ideals, about the meaning of culture, about spiritual and intellectual values. He was personally interested in me.

A modern classroom is also a little parliament where competition, rather than co-operation or fellowship, is learned. The future citizens are trained to fight each for himself in life; they are penalized for helping a friend in difficulty, and in the obsession for individual marks they are taught the jealousy of rivals.

One teacher in Neuchâtel recently tried out a system of grading by groups. At first it was resented by the good students, who were angered because they were no longer able to stand out from the others. Soon, however, he saw them devise ways of pushing the weaker students so that the team results would be improved!

One of my friends walked the corridors of the federal legislature during several sessions, getting to know the deputies and showing interest in them and in their life and cares. He was able to see how these men, so busy and so close to one another, remained alone with their personal problems. Yet these problems exercise a real repercussion upon their moods and their decisions in the House. He invited two deputies from different parties to lunch with him. He noticed that these adversaries, who had for years debated so many grave problems in parliament and in committees, had never met each other in private, and were quite surprised that they felt so close and so alike once they had talked together man to man.

This disassociation between the function and the man is the very essence of what I call the parliamentary spirit.

Each one has a function, and in the play of social life he fulfills his role, which is completely apart from his person. What would unite the two would be precisely those human relationships which are disregarded. What divides us is our function, the interests which we " represent." One can see the same idea at first upheld by friends of its author and attacked by his adversaries, and later taken up by the adversaries only to be attacked by the friends. Confronted with a project, an experiment, or a doctrine, the first consideration is to discover where it came from. A label is put on each man. He is obliged to look upon himself as representing only a fraction of the country. Woe to the man who tries to remain objective and to maintain a wide perspective: everyone will label him as an enemy! We are interested in people's ideas, but not in the people.

For four years I took part in the governing body of my church. With the aggressive spirit that I had, I threw myself into the debates with great zeal. Later on, some of my former colleagues came to see me privately. I discovered a degree of moral suffering in them that I had never suspected at the time when my only concern was the influence their ideas might exercise for or against mine. Then I felt I was of more service to my church by showing affection for them and helping them to solve their personal problems than by all my former arguing.

It is this same parliamentary spirit, this same disassociation between the person and his role, which has led to the modern dogma that a man's private life is of no concern and bears no weight in his professional or political career. And so we see a man who lives immorally drawing up laws for the protection of the family, another who is incapable of self-discipline in his personal expenses regulating the state's budget, and a third who is at war with his wife called upon to re-establish social accord.

In Switzerland, democracy had a personal character for many centuries — it was founded by men who had met together in the presence of God and had sworn mutual help. In our small towns, the citizens knew one another. Just as in the tradition preserved in our cantonal churches, they all came together and saw with their eyes and heard with their ears the candidates that they were to choose. For them, the candidates were real persons, not just names on printed programs.

Oh, I know that there were some serious clashes, but today if our citizens show less interest in public affairs, it is not surprising. For they are buried in paper, in abstraction and party anonymity. In the smallest district, instead of assembling the electors, speaking to them and letting them speak, they are made to enter the poll booth in strict privacy and deposit a printed list of names.

We can bring thousands together for a sports event, talk to them all by means of the loud-speaker, and have them share the same emotions. But the parliamentary spirit has so succeeded that one sees the church, which ought to have the sense of fellowship, imitating the state in servile fashion with its secret ballot, its little committee, its stamps, and its private poll booth into which the few dozen voters file.

I would like to propose an amendment to the federal constitution to the following effect: " No one can elect someone whom he does not know."

Ours is a juridical civilization, an economist used to tell me, where everything is done on paper and where a League of Nations is exhausted while seeking a definition for peace and war. In an equally juridical age, Seneca called for a return from theory to life itself and held that the personal influence of leaders was more important than their doctrines.

It is striking to note that the authority of the International Committee of the Red Cross has held together amidst the breakdown of all international law to the same extent precisely that it has avoided the parliamentary spirit. Conferences of the International Red Cross bring together delegates from every nation, as is customary. The International Committee, however, has been constituted from its very beginning as a veritable team — one might even say a group of friends — chosen for their personal merit and commitment, not as representatives of various factions. In this way, even though made up exclusively of Swiss men, it has preserved a much more international spirit than any parliamentary organism such as the council of the League of Nations, where the seats were carefully awarded according to the importance of each nation.

In our Switzerland, both our federal and cantonal constitutions have wisely laid down the principle of a collegial-type government. Generally, people believe that the unity of the team depends upon one party's having a majority of the members. Rather, it is just to the extent that the members of the government are chosen for their personal qualities and that their party, the district they represent, and their religious affiliation are forgotten that the best strands within our national tradition are followed.

II

It is especially in the social realm that I would like to show the influence of this parliamentary spirit. The greatest social problem today is that the worker is no longer conscious either of being a person or of the possibility of being a person, a whole man. He counts only for the position he fills, the work he can do, or the political power that he represents. This has been forcefully expressed in our country by C. F. Ducommun, the former railroad worker who was for a long time an enthusiast for Marxian doctrine but who now is courageously working for the coming of a Christian social policy. He has put it in this way (in *La Suisse forge son destin*): "The worker feels reduced, in the attitude of certain employers, to the status of being simply an element in the cost of production. . . . The worker has been 'disintegrated' by the industrial revolution of the machine age and, if Marxianism has found favor with him, it is because it attempted to provide him with a philosophy which was religious, political, and economic, at the same time. It offered the worker a total view of the world and its destiny. . . . Man had a goal, even though this was false and illusory."

Today, when the Marxian illusion is being shattered, the worker needs to regain his place in industry as a human being. This may be possible through means of an industrial fellowship of Christian inspiration which, in order to be not just another little parliament, will have to be not just a juridical organization but a reform in both employer's and employee's thinking.

One day an old and retired French officer came to consult with me. We had a long talk. He had known Clemenceau and had spoken to him of his theory concerning the social problem. His theory struck me as remarkable: In any organism, there are both motor and sensory nerves. If the motor nerves are always transmitting orders from the brain to the various parts of the body, the sensory nerves are also continually bringing back information and feelings to the brain. Well, this reciprocity shown in nature does not exist in industry. There is a one-way street; there are but orders from above to those below. The worker is not asked for his opinion. In the shop, he sees plenty of things that could be organized differently in order to improve production, but he is not asked for his suggestions. His qualities of intelligence, personality, and co-operation do not count; he is only a producer, a cog in the wheel that executes orders. Often the worker knows more than his boss, and yet the more the boss is incompetent the more he abuses his authority to silence his subordinates lest his ignorance be shown.

The first worker with whom I became quite close — because we opened up completely to each other — told me how he had worked in France during the war of 1914. A protégé of the firm's associate director had been fitted in there in charge of the inspection of finished products. However, since he did not know that such a thing as a caliper square existed, he used a monkey wrench for measuring! It is this sort of incompetence which inflicts the deepest wounds upon the workers.

Quite recently, I treated a sprained ankle, an accident that happened in construction. Now, I no longer have any time for treating accidents and the like, but the man was one of my oldest clients. It was also an opportunity for me to realize how the simplest-looking case can be full of instruction on the human problem. It is not necessary that the case be a formal one, in which the patient has come to me to tell of his problems because I have written a book that inspires his confidence.

For the compensation record, my client simply said that he had slipped at work. I questioned him a bit further. " The foreman is unfit," he answered. " There was a large ditch, dug out of clay soil. I told him we'd need a ladder, but he laughed at me. So I cut out some steps, but — it all caved in. My buddy thought I was going to break my neck. I don't want to complain against the foreman, since I'm covered by workmen's compensation. . . ." How the compensation helps to shut the worker's mouth! I pressed him further: " Can't you talk to him tactfully, so that he'll learn something from this? " " Of course not! " answered the patient. " I'd be let off tomorrow."

Many employers tell us that the very best spirit prevails in their firm, that they have a fine paternal relationship with their workers. Passing through the workshop, they politely ask, " How is it going? " And the worker answers respectfully, " Fine, sir." They are unaware that a certain conventional decorum, to which they are too habituated, has to be broken in order that a true human relationship be established between them and their workers.

A certain girl worked in a small shop. Every year her supervisor asked her very politely, " Would such and such a time be convenient for you to take your holidays? " For ten years the unchanging answer was, " Why, yes, ma'am." Once, however, she hesitantly said, " It would be a real help to me if they could start a week later." The reply was immediate: " Oh, no! It's impossible. It's all arranged already! " The supervisor's seemingly polite consultation was but a formula.

An officer told me that the first thing he realized after his promotion to captain was that none of the orders he received were executable in the manner in which they were formulated. The orders did not take into account the conditions under which the unit's commander had to work.

Understand me well — this is no plea for an overthrow of authority. Fellowship does not mean disorder, but the opposite. There is no question of the higher officer's ceasing to give orders, of the employer's surrendering his leadership responsibilities into the hands of his personnel, or of the father's abdicating all authority in the home. It is easy to see that it is precisely those parents who have thus given up their burden as educators who have become strangers to their children. It is rather a question of re-establishing human bonds and this two-way flow of communication of which my officer friend spoke to Clemenceau. Each person needs to feel that he shares in a common task and to see the problems that others are facing, so as to be able to understand their decisions and to accomplish more fully the task he has at his level.

Thus, with relation to the social organization of business, three distinct conceptions face us: (1) the patriarchal or classical authoritative system, wherein the boss gives the orders and the personnel are expected to execute orders received without using their intelligence; (2) the communist conception, which weakens the essential order by attempting to give to the personnel the functions of leadership. Unfortunately, this is the system so many think of when they talk about re-establishing a human bond between boss and worker; (3) the organic conception, which is as different from the first as from the second, in which there is re-created the spirit of fellowship through face-to-face relationships, without for a moment introducing any confusion as to respective functions and levels of authority. For long it seemed that our only choice was between the first two alternatives. Because of their fears of getting involved in the errors of the communist conception, many employers have clung to the patriarchal system and have carefully kept their distance from their workers. I should like to convince them that there is a third way, which will restore the dignity and human worth of the worker and strengthen both his professional proficiency and his interest in and attachment to the business as well, without the employers' having to abdicate their responsibilities of direction.

It's a question of getting to know the person, of being interested in the person more than in his ideas. C. F. Ducommun mentions (in *La Suisse forge son destin*) " a manager . . . who invited the workers to his home, in groups of twenty-five. In less than three months he had in this way come to know his six hundred employees. These contacts are renewed continually, bringing with them better solutions to the problems of the common task."

Mr. Ducommun describes those employers who find a great, creative adventure in directing their firms, seeking markets, and facing the risks of competition, but whose workers know nothing of this. The workers are forced to satisfy their need for adventure on the weekend, or in sports. Yet a whole new interest for their work is born in them when they understand the problems that face the entire firm.

Often they do not even see the finished machine into which the part that they produce goes, and they know nothing of what goes on in the other departments. In one factory, the staff organized a tour of the shops and offices for all the employees and their families. It took place on a Saturday afternoon. It turned out to be a real eye opener for most, and a good party as well, when they came to know one another.

It's a matter of mutual understanding, of being interested in one another, of each considering the other.

Dr. André Missenard, a student of the effect of climatic conditions upon factory output, has written, "If we had earlier been concerned with the men and not just the machinery, we would have long been able to measure the harmful influence of these conditions upon the output of our man power."

How many parents who demand respect from their children show respect for these same children? Here is a boy who has a great need to work off his energy. I ask what he does on Sunday. His father won't let him leave the back yard, but neither will he let him make any noise because the father, tired out by the week's work, wants to sleep in peace on the garden chair.

Weatherhead mentions the father whose family often respectfully waits for him to finish a task before serving dinner but who, in return, demands that his son come immediately, although he could as easily say to him, " John, as soon as your tower of blocks is finished, come and eat like a nice boy." Neither authority nor true discipline would be lost thereby.

It is a question of respecting one another. "In every man," writes Dr. Théo. Bovet, "we respect the divinely created being."

It is a question of ceasing to fear one another. Because he fears his pupils, the teacher deals severely with them. It is because the foreman fears his workers — that is, he fears being shown to know less than they on a given point — that he cuts off every discussion with them and finds refuge in silence. He invokes the accepted authority of the boss to terminate an agreement that might embarrass him. Again, for fear of his wife's criticism, a husband will hide the little gift he has bought himself and which he has secretly coveted for a long time.

All of us are constantly holding two conversations. The outer conversation deals with the serious subjects — discussions on great principles or, for example, interviews that I have with patients. At the same time there is the inner conversation, which deals with smaller matters, matters which we hold dear to us: "Will I be late for my next appointment? Will my wife be in a better mood when I get home? What would the doctor think of me if he knew what I said to her when I left home this morning?" Or again, "Would my client lose confidence in me if I admitted to him that I don't understand his case at all and that his questions embarrass me greatly?"

Nevertheless, as Dr. Dubois has put it, that which helps the patient the most is to discover that he "is not so far off from us as he thinks he is. . . . Stretch out our hand to him. . . . Let us not be afraid of admitting to him our own failings, our inborn flaws; let us draw closer to him."

What isolates the patient the most in his life — whether schoolboy, housewife, or worker — is the very thing that isolates us the most: our secrets.

Here is a young woman who as an adolescent was her brothers' confidante. The secrets of their moral conflicts, which they entrusted to her, were too heavy for their sister, who couldn't unload them elsewhere, their parents being sick. She has been literally crushed by them.

III

It is our own secrets, however, that separate us the most from others: remorse for our wrongdoings, fears that haunt us, disgust with ourselves that we continually succumb to a certain recurring temptation, inner doubts so vividly in contrast with our air of self-confidence, our jealousy and our anger, and even the naïve daydreams of glory by which we console ourselves.

When people open up to us, we discover that their real remorse has to do with faults quite different from those for which others reproach them. Others aim criticism at their failings, but their own accusations are aimed at a deeper level of conscience, at the sin that is as a hidden source of their visible failings. At the level of their failings, we succeed only in humiliating them, for their great desire is to be free from these although they never succeed in freeing themselves; at the level of sin, we can lead them into the experience of liberation.

No one finds it easy to overcome the inner resistance that obstructs the way to a sincere and deep unveiling of himself.

People come to me, thinking they've found a man who finds interpersonal relationships relatively easy. They can hardly believe me when I tell them it's just the opposite. As a child, I was terribly withdrawn. Orphaned quite young, I withdrew into my own lonely little world, even though I was treated kindly. My daydreams and secret projects only isolated me more from the others. Whenever I met a group of pals, they would change their conversation, out of embarrassment. I felt I was of no importance to anyone and that no one was really interested in me. One day I entered the living room quietly and realized that I was the subject of the discussion. It was an upheaval in my young soul; I could hardly believe it possible.

I rather think that if I've chosen medicine, it was a bit by instinct, desiring to find a springboard in this profession to help me overcome the hurdle of my overpowering sense of loneliness and, also, to penetrate into the mysteries of life about which I had never dared to question anyone.

Later on as a doctor, I still remained aloof, impersonal, inscrutable. My profession was not healing me; my sickness was obstructing my vocation, bringing me deep disappointment.

Over ten years ago, when a friend challenged me to put into practice the Christian faith I professed, the first step that came clearly to my mind was to unburden myself completely to my wife of many thoughts, memories, fears, and failures, which I had never mentioned to her. Such a step seemed impossible to me. I felt I would lose her confidence. We had been very close, and loved each other deeply. We used to discuss everything, even religion. I used to develop for her my pet theories, and she would express admiration and approval. But it is one thing to speak on the level of ideas, and it is an altogether different thing to speak of one's own soul. When I took this step, my wife answered me, " Then I *can* be of some help to you! " And she opened up to me in return. We had found the meaning of fellowship. She told me, " Up till now you've been my doctor, my psychologist, my chaplain, more than my husband." In my zeal to help her in her life, my professional vocation had come to hide the person of her husband. It humiliated her by making her into a " case " rather than a wife, and it hindered her personality from coming into full bloom. I have known several colleagues whose marriages have been hindered by this same obstacle, sometimes with grave results, which, fortunately, had not been the case with us.

This upheaval in our relationships with others, of which I have spoken here, is achieved by no one in his professional and social relationships unless he first experiences it with his closest fellow — his father, his brother, or his wife.

A client of mine all of a sudden made the remark, " Ah, women! What a queer type of mechanism! " Yes, in fact they are in most homes a mystery to their husbands. The husband does not realize what an amazing wonder he has beside him, which he could discover if he approached her without his preconceived ideas and if he dared to begin by revealing his own inner mechanism.

I can recall when I was on the highway with a friend a few days after his confession to me. He was quite bothered. "Do you think I should talk about it to my wife? Won't it upset her too much?" He wanted me to make his decision, but I am always careful to allow people to follow their own sense of leading. That same evening his home became a real fellowship, whose outgoing influence has steadily grown through the years.

I recall a young woman who, after a difficult confession, and without my even mentioning her husband, suddenly blurted out, "I could never tell that to my husband!" I recall, too, the joy on her face a few months later when she told me she had taken that step.

A colleague had just proudly shown me a beautiful ophthalmoscope that he had bought. We had each looked into one end of the apparatus, and we had each been able to see right to the bottom of the other's eye, taking in all its details. Then his wife came into the room and I felt his sudden withdrawing within himself. I looked at the ophthalmoscope on the desk and I thought of what relaxing of tensions might take place if only each of them could look into the depths of the other's soul.

Happy are those couples who share this experience even before marriage.

However, how many there are who, favored by their mutual love, begin thus in an absolute loyalty to each other. And then, almost imperceptibly, they draw apart. They think they will preserve their love by ceasing to be frank with the one they love, and this very lack of honesty compromises their love. The husband sees no reason why he should shake his wife's trust by telling of the warm feeling he had while meeting a young woman, or by sharing with her his troubled conscience over a little connivance in accounting that he has used in order to meet a payment deadline! She would take these harmless things too seriously. She would worry for nothing and become suspicious of all his actions.

It is precisely because there is a secret that her trust is no longer the same. She questions him. Her questioning only causes him to withdraw farther. He parries it by little lies. When she discovers a lie, the wife becomes more suspicious and harries him more with her questioning. He is caught in his little lies more often and, because of the difficulties of business that don't work out as he had hoped, temptations gain a greater hold over him. He is obliged to lie more often. His wife tells the doctor, "I no longer can trust my husband at all." Yet she loves him and would still save him. The feeling of having let his wife down paralyzes the husband with regard to his wife. He finds her irritating, with an air of superiority as if she alone knows how to act aright.

Many times a husband, somewhat weak in character, seeks an escape in order to hide his failings, but the well-intentioned zeal of the virtuous wife only widens the gulf between them. Or, a husband and wife may lower their ideals of marriage and fall back upon tact: I won't meddle with your personal affairs and neither will you meddle with mine.

However, the situation can be straightened out by the entrance of a new quality of trust. There are, in fact, two types of trust. One is that naïve and human trust based on the other's merits. Such is the trust of the young bride who believes her husband faultless. Bit by bit, life picks away at this trust with each succeeding disappointment. Then there is supernatural trust, that which we put in others when we open up to them, which we put in them because of their very weakness, instead of strength. The first kind is spoken of by those who say, " I've been deceived so many times that I can no longer trust anyone." It is upon the second kind that a ministry of love can be built that trusts a man in order to help him straighten out his life. For it is when we find such trust in a friend that we speak freely and thus break the bonds of our emotional solitude.

The obstacle to trust is always the lack of love or of loyalty. To say a few encouraging words that we don't believe ourselves, to pretend to love more than we really do, this only leads the other into a deeper discouragement.

Now, I must be sincere toward my reader and admit that I've met couples for whom a sincere confession, instead of bringing them together, only created a barrier between them for a long time. There is the man who, having just come into contact with the idea of absolute frankness, immediately told his wife the whole story of his family and money, which he had hitherto kept to himself. It only drew them apart. The reason for such failure seems to me to be that the climate of love, in which sincerity can be supported, had not first been created. It is as if we wanted an orange sapling to support a full-grown fruit: the branch would break.

The doctor, like the gardener, learns to wait. He has a biological view of the soul's growth and he knows that each event has its time, which must not be hurried or retarded.

Elsewhere I have told the story of a marital conflict in the life of a patient whose case I followed for years. After a spiritual experience he was exercised by an inner calling to seek reconciliation with his wife. Yet, I didn't feel him to be ready for that. I gave him no encouragement because, as long as there is a need to defend oneself, the "explanations" only spoil things that they are intended to remedy. For a long time he receded from the initial desire, until one day he was ready for the harvest of reconciliation. And it was wonderful. This patient died a few months later, completely happy, and left an unchangeable memory of this joy to his wife.

In every case I notice more and more that whether they are defeated or very strong, all men lack confidence in themselves. Thus they all have an immense need that others trust them.

"What is trust?" writes Dr. Axel Munthe. "Where does it originate? in the head or in the heart?"

Like him, I think that it is from the heart and that it is a gift of God. Thus it is that in placing themselves in the presence of God, man and wife can regain such trust in spite of all the hindrances.

III

The Spirit of Independence

I

There is a second area in which the mentality of our age opposes a restoration of the experience of fellowship. This is found in the individualistic philosophy in which, ever since Descartes, we have been immersed.

I am always amazed when I realize to what degree millions of people actually determine their whole way of thinking, feeling, and engaging in practical action from the philosophy of a man whose writings, centuries old, they have never read.

It was a curious illusion of the nineteenth century to think that the time for philosophical speculations had definitely ended and that, thanks to the introduction of positive methods, men would henceforth be spiritually free. This amounted actually to the creating of a new metaphysic without realizing it. Thus a whole train of new prejudices was introduced into the history of thought, prejudices from which our contemporaries have difficulty in freeing themselves.

The same is true with regard to the individualistic conceptions introduced by the Renaissance and later set forth by Descartes's rationalist methodology. Our age is still steeped in it. I am not exaggerating here. Even though I proclaim in this writing that a true solution to the crisis of our civilization demands a restoration of the meaning of fellowship, and I believe this, yet my personal reactions are still those of an individualist.

Of course, we always preach to ourselves when we preach to others, in order to bring ourselves farther along in what we believe to be the right direction, but against which all our education and training is opposed. One of my ministerial friends, for example, never loses a chance to call for the restoration of authority within the church; yet he has the greatest difficulty in submitting personally to authority.

We can hope that after us, future generations will have been awakened to the need of fellowship from their childhood up, and that this will be as natural for them as our fierce independence is for us.

It is not the writings of a philosopher that really count, as much as it is the total evolving mind of the age, which he has reflected, but which both deforms and goes beyond his thought. Such is the case with Descartes.

Descartes was a believer. His ambition apparently was to crown his philosophical system with an apologetic for Christianity. Unfortunately, the Queen of Sweden, by her capricious demands, brought him down to a premature grave. In his mind, reason could never supplant faith. "An atheist," he wrote, "cannot be a geometrician, for he cannot believe in his diagrams if he does not first believe in God." Nevertheless, by claiming to admit nothing as certain except what could be proved so by reason, Descartes started human thought off in the direction that was to separate it more and more from the authority of revelation. The Cartesian proofs of God's existence were to fall under the blows of Cartesian logic used by men who no longer held Descartes's faith!

Just as surely as in Descartes's century the individualistic ardor of the Renaissance had been passed, so it was just in order to unite men in a community of thought that the philosopher proposed a rigorous methodology that they might all faithfully accept as a common rule. Yet, his appeal that each accept only what his reason could take as evident is the very thing that has made individualism something sacred in the Western world for three centuries now.

With Descartes, the individual has been made the first reality. He proves his own existence first of all, completely independently of all external contingencies that are his, and then he approaches the study of the external world in terms of his own individual existence.

We constantly think and act as if our own life were absolutely autonomous, at least in principle, and independent of God who created it, of the surrounding world into which it was born, and of the human community without which it is inconceivable. [We continually think and act as if we possessed by right an absolute sovereignty, and as if the community's claims upon us were based only on concessions we have willingly made. It is as if we made concessions for the sake of our common life while at the same time retaining the right of withdrawal.]

The best illustration that we have of this mentality is to be found in the relationships between our Swiss cantons, which have remained, essentially, absolutely sovereign states. Our federation may be described as negative; its power consists only in those powers which the cantons have been happy to delegate, according to their own pleasure. We all know how such a federal system has prevented the birth of a national mind in Switzerland. The same situation is true in international relations, only much more so, because of the dogma of the absolute sovereignty of states. As long as this dogma survives, the appearance of a world community will be made impossible.

I have no intention of minimizing the good that has resulted from our Swiss Federation, of which Denis de Rougemont has written so effectively, showing what our system could do for the solving of international problems. Nevertheless, it is obvious that our proponents of a negative type of federation have a bitter and morose attitude toward all the progress made on the federal level, which they resent as so much godless infringement upon cantonal sovereignty.

In the same way in our individualistic point of view, those who consider themselves as essentially independent resent all the practical demands of the common life. They regard as so much sacrifice, or even personal offense, the fact that they cannot eat at the hour that pleases them, dress according to their fancy, flout the rules of politeness, or flirt with whoever pleases them, without their parents' or marital partner's interference.

Rousseau's idea of the social contract has also contributed to the modern individualistic conception of society. In him we see the same paradox as in Descartes. Though an individualist in his personal life, Rousseau did not intend to preach individualism when he developed the concept of the social contract, because he saw this as the total alienation of all the rights of each associate in favor of the community. Nonetheless, this concept of society, with which we are all saturated, has resulted in our seeing its only validity as a kind of conditional power of attorney of our sovereign individual rights.

Of course, the spirit of independence was not born in modern times. Men have always found it hard to submit to the demands of social life. "Society is a bringing together of wild beasts," wrote Seneca. Before him, Heraclitus of Ephesus had claimed that everything was the result of a "conflict of opposites," and made "war . . . the father of all things."

The particular characteristic of modern individualism is that, instead of considering this universal conflict a social disease, it is seen as the normal and necessary condition of existence. Heraclitus taught "the unity of all things," and Seneca added to his pessimistic remark, "Thus the wise person . . . will look upon men just as favorably disposed as a doctor looks upon his patients." Modern man, on the contrary, defends his independence in the face of others' demands and society's infringements and does not consider himself sick, but rather in legitimate defense of his rights.

Machiavelli contributed much to this with his theory of society as "only the play of human powers and the conflict of passions." Voltaire, too, who saw in "self-love . . . a prerequisite for social life," has influenced us, as has Schopenhauer with his remark, "It is boredom which has brought it about that

beings which care for each other as little as men do, nevertheless seek each other's company."

With Ibsen, upon whom we were raised in our youth, this
glorification of the individual reached its peak. Like Nietzsche,
he held that "the strongest man is the loneliest man."

All of this is worthless for our Western civilization in full
crisis. India has preserved its sense of the spiritual values that
the individual achieves in communion with the totality of being. In Japan's paper houses, what we call "private life" does
not exist. In the West, on the other hand, a philosophy of "each
man for himself" is all-powerful, flattering the inborn pride of
men and isolating and setting them one against the other as
much in their thinking as in their life, be it political, economic,
or social. We can mention the medical profession, plagued as it
is with the spirit of competition, as one example. In this regard,
Dr. Vincent has raised a resounding cry of alarm.

Since I've mentioned medicine, let me point out that the individualistic concept of society coincided with the cellular
theory in which the human organism was seen as a series of
individual cells, much as various parts go together to make a
machine. Likewise, the rebirth of comprehensive medicine,
that is, Hippocratic medicine, which recognizes the fundamental unity of the organism and the absolute interdependence of
all its parts, coincides with the present need to rediscover the
meaning of social fellowship.

Modern science has sought in vain a specific quality of living
matter. The characteristic of life is found neither in the chemical make-up of the molecule, vitamin, or hormone, which can
be synthesized in the laboratory, nor yet in physicochemical
reactions, studied individually. This is why life has evaded all
analysis. What does characterize life is its organization; it is the
mutual relationship of individual elements obviously ordered
for the purpose of a common existence.

Thus science forces us to see how contrary to nature itself is
that philosophy which was the byword of our youth: "Live
your own life!" To live one's own life in complete autonomy,

unrestricted by those evident organic relationships which tie us to our milieu, is to deny life itself. As a matter of fact, those who pursue this ideal live to see dry up within themselves that vitality which comes only from dialogue with one's surroundings.

The patients whom we see every day consider themselves free to obey or disobey our instructions, as they please. If we prescribe a potion, they generally take it if it doesn't taste too bad. However, when we touch upon what needs changing in their life — their self-containedness or their immorality — they exclaim, " Ask me anything you want, doctor, but not that! " And they add, " After all, I'm free to behave the way I like. That's my own business, since I'm the one who will take the consequences." Is that so? The laws of heredity, of social interdependence, of suggestibility, and of moral contagion are such that none of our gestures, actions, or thoughts are free from consequences quite outside ourselves, consequences that we can no longer control.

I do not need to point out that I see many sick and " well " whose personal lives and social relationships are altogether poisoned by the spirit of independence and contradiction.

Here is a young man who shares his father's profession. So ardently does he want to live his own life and owe nothing to his father that he has serious inhibitions in his work, and he fails to profit from paternal experience and counsel.

Here is a very intelligent girl, so jealous of her independence that she has refused to take a step necessary for her career. She fears the indiscreet questions of her mother that would come if she took the step. She doesn't want to have to give any answers. When I asked her, " If you had a daughter, would you want her to hide her life from you? " she lowered her head.

Here is a husband who asserts his freedom in such fashion as to deny the meaning of marriage: " So long as I'm not unfaithful to my wife with other women, she has no say in my affairs." And to emphasize his freedom and his independence from the wife's questioning, he behaves in a manner that doesn't conform even to his ideal.

Here is a very cultured man, four times divorced, who is in conflict with his present wife. When I asked if it was he who had always asked for the divorce, he replied, " Why, of course! " with such a proud tone that I felt his complete assumption that he was free to do what he liked with himself. He has always obtained his wives' consent and cannot now accept the fact that his present wife is opposed to it. Besides, he has a certain nobility of soul and refuses to force his wife to consent. Hence he is full of self-pity that he is not able to act in complete freedom. Yet, he secretly feels the need of fellowship, for he has come to see me and has shown complete trust in me.

Of course, that is a tendency from which no man is exempt. What I want to point out, however, is that the spirit of our age aggravates this revolt against all constraint. Marriage is a bond. True marriage is a total bond, a complete renunciation of personal independence. This is enough in itself that many men think that they can no longer love the one whom they are henceforth sworn to love. For them, love cannot be other than spontaneous, and for this reason it withers as soon as it becomes an obligation.

Another person, a married woman, wonders whom she would marry if her husband died. By this she shows clearly her claim to independence. Since she is married she is no longer free to choose whom she will love, but this she has never, deep down, accepted. She dreams of being once more free in her choice. This is the denial of love as a bond; it becomes instead the exaltation of individual emotion.

I see many people who seem ashamed of consulting me. " I've always wanted to straighten things out by myself," they say — as if it were ever possible to straighten things out by oneself! Alone, a person gets more hopelessly entangled. As if I had ever been able to solve a really personal problem without passing through the narrow gate of confession and the humiliating admission of my inability to straighten myself out alone!

This same feeling is often a stumbling block to faith and

piety. To many it seems that they would be cowardly to turn to God in their distress. They would like to solve all their problems themselves first of all and then offer to God the services of a victor. Naturally, this beautiful epic never takes place.

The pride of independence is the greatest temptation for the more talented people. To tell the truth, we often feel like damning their brilliance, their abilities, their incontestable merit, which has turned them into this blind alley of thinking that they can work out all things without needing anyone's help. Their brilliance, their abilities, and even their merit become sterile because of the isolation into which these qualities have thrown them. It is painful to see how many persons there are who are richly endowed morally and intellectually — and yes, even spiritually — whose lives are all but useless as far as being fruitful is concerned, and who are only the more distressed that they feel in themselves such great possibilities. It often makes me angry, for it all seems so stupid. Their wounded self-respect only strengthens their fierce independence, the very cause of their sterility.

Ch. Beaudoin has written that " there are none like the men of genius to prove incapable of understanding one another."

II

Here we come in contact with one of the first paradoxes present in this problem of the spirit of independence — often it is a question of those who are rich not only in intelligence or strength of will but also in affection. It is readily seen that those who are the most distant and withdrawn, those who have the greatest difficulty in integrating themselves into a group, are the very ones with the greatest affective needs and the greatest thirst for human fellowship. They are looked upon as icicles, but when they dare to open up, we realize what a warm heart they have, burning with the desire to love and be loved.

I can think of a certain deaconess, for instance, extremely shy, who always feels strange in her community, and yet she more than any other needs and wants to feel herself a part of it. It is precisely the intensity of her desire that robs her of spontaneity and paralyzes her when she is with her sister deaconesses.

The fear of being alone thrusts us into independence, for fear creates what it fears. The fear of famine leads to war and war leads to famine. Stephen Foot has written some pages on this subject, full of insight: " It is astonishing when we realize to what degree fear dictates to most men and women in the ordinary activities of daily life." He applies this to the life of nations as well: " The fear of war, the fear of attack, the fear for security — these are the things which build up walls of incomprehension between nations, creating an atmosphere favorable to war. The fear of war can produce war."

A second paradox is that our century, which has lost the sense of community and has glorified the individual, has been so poor in great personalities. Denis de Rougemont has convincingly established this fact. Actually, the opposition that we constantly make between the person and the community is illusory. Those who become creative and original personalities are not the ones who live their own lives, but those who forget themselves in giving themselves for others.

If we speak here of rediscovering the sense of fellowship, the reader will understand that this does not mean following the crowd unthinkingly or conforming to the fad. Actually, the desire to live one's own life is only a fad. " Dare to step aside from the crowd that would drag you along with it," wrote Romain Rolland. " Every man who would be truly a man must learn to remain himself when in the crowd, and to think for himself on behalf of all, and at times, in spite of all," said Beaudoin. Yes! " On behalf of all " — this is the cornerstone of the spirit of fellowship.

A third paradox is that the people most jealous of their independence are the most authoritarian in their dealings with others. This can be easily observed. Though unable to submit to the most moderate authority, they impose their own will most inflexibly upon anyone who becomes subject to them. The explanation of this paradox is that both these reactions are compensations for doubts regarding themselves. Those who feel strong are not always on the defensive with their superiors and have no need to growl at their inferiors.

A fourth paradox is that the very age which has elevated the individual has given the least consideration to man's personal value within the context of his public and social functions. This I have shown already.

A fifth paradox is that our age, which has committed the individual to repulse any outside interference, is also the age of so few really free minds. This fact is very striking with regard to faith. A freethinker such as Dr. Dubois, of Bern, has stated this quite honestly by remarking that very few freethinkers think freely. They are slaves of the atheistic bias they have adopted. Here is a patient whose mother, having been raised in a church orphanage, and disgusted by a cold ritualism, has reacted by espousing atheism. She raised her child in this attitude and took him along to the free-thought meetings. And now he realizes that there he was stuffed with clichés far more than he could have been in any church. In order to eliminate the idea of a Creator, the freethinkers developed theories of the infinity and eternity of the universe that my patient now recognizes to be just as hypothetical as any theory of God. He had never heard of Pascal's wager, which I mentioned to him!

Thus the crowd have been aroused to win a supposed spiritual independence by rejecting the authority of revelation. In their dismay they become the playthings of the day's thousand and one suggestions, following those ideologies which are the most bereft of real thought, those doctrines which are the most fanatic, those idols which are the most meaningless — money, the printed word, and sexual pleasure.

The moral strength is sapped in this glorification of freedom. People are beginning to realize with the philosopher Spir that freedom is found only in the good and ceases to exist in the evil.

A last paradox is that the men who defend their independence the most stubbornly really are not free at all in practice.

They depend upon their spirit of contradiction. I see, for example, many young people who are revolting against parental authority. In this way, so they think, they will hammer out their freedom. Instead of that, when there is a decision to take it is predetermined by their systematic opposition, whereas, if they followed their own convictions, they might find themselves sometimes in agreement with their parents. Psychologically, they depend completely upon their parents even while they are at war with them. This is really not so paradoxical, since their revolt against parental authority is only the projection of discontent with themselves for not daring to become truly free. When we fear life, it is easier to be persuaded that our failure to confront it stems from outside interference than it is to admit that we lack the necessary courage.

Most teen-agers suffer from a child complex that they manage to conceal from themselves by their demand for independence. He who is inwardly truly free acts in that freedom, instead of complaining about others' intruding authority.

There are two ways " to be oneself," according to this familiar expression. There is the negative way of revolt, contradiction, refusal to obey, and complaining. This weakens the group and does nothing to strengthen the person. Then there is the positive affirmation of self, which unwittingly comes from serving the larger group. The man who, instead of worrying about defending his person, brings his thought and creative activity into the group, becomes a leader, a strong personality.

After a child has long been dominated by his parents — say for thirty, forty, or even sixty years, having passively conformed to their way of life, thought, and action — sometimes he must for a while pass through an acute phase of negative self-affirmation. However, if he remains thus, it is because his long dependence has sown the seed of self-doubt in his heart.

Here is a young woman, with a marked inferiority complex, who has been completely dependent on her parents, behind whom she could hide her weakness from her brothers and sisters, whom she feared. Now she has begun to awaken to a personal life and dares to stick up for her own ideas, which has brought continual and bitter argument into the home. Certain families expect that one of their members will be completely passive, and they are all upset if he begins to show his own conviction. It is taken as impertinence and self-importance. He is accused of having broken the family's unity, although such unity can in reality exist only in the full development of each person. It is completely overlooked that this contradiction is an appeal for a higher kind of unity founded upon affection rather than upon servile acquiescence.

All men, even in their most tumultuous conflicts, their loneliest periods of despondency, and their most meaningless diversions, reveal therein, to those who have eyes to see, how much they long for real fellowship. "This is why we like noise and movement so much," wrote Pascal, "why prison is such a terrible punishment, and why the love of solitude is incomprehensible. The greatest element of felicity in royal life is that the kings' servants are constantly trying to amuse them and procure every kind of pleasure for them."

I treated a young man who from his adolescence had been cut off from social life by sickness. Gifted with real literary talent, he poured out his heart into the writing of theatrical plays. In one of them the hero had himself written a stirring tragedy during a prolonged illness. From the very first production, this play won the public's acclaim. Yet, in the triumph of success, the author felt himself foreign to the adoring crowd and withdrew into himself once again, bitter, to live in his ivory tower. I saw in this his tremendous hunger for reintegration into society. When my friend accomplished this, he was able to tell me that if he could write the play over, he would give it an altogether different ending.

Nothing is more contagious than joy; however, he who while in the midst of a happy group does not feel at one with them, who is not carried along by their contagious spirit, is plunged into an even deeper despondency. Yet, this despondency betrays his very despair at having remained an outsider.

Every man fears this, and this is the very thing that drives him into conflict. "If we win," said Joseph Goebbels on February 19, 1943, "everyone will want to be our friend, but if we were to lose, we could count our friends on the fingers of one hand." There is a different way to build the bridges of fellowship than that of imposing fellowship by force. It is the way marked out by Christ, the way of love.

III

The need for fellowship is inescapable because it is inscribed in nature. "We were born to live together," wrote Seneca. "Our society is an arch of stones joined together, which would break down if each did not support the other." Those perfected animal societies, wherein instinct guides each individual in the precise role he must fulfill for the good of the group, are a proof of this. Try to preach individualism to the ants and the bees!

The socially unintegrated fall into an exaggerated self-analysis, as one of my patients pointed out to me, from which they no longer can free themselves and that makes them suffer even more. They are thus driven farther from human fellowship.

They fall into faultfinding. Here is a young lady in a fine professional career, who is yet actually quite alone as a result of some major disappointments. She expresses her bitterness through her deep and penetrating criticism of everything — her work, her boss, her family, her community, and her church. Naturally, with such an attitude a renewing of personal ties is impossible.

Also, the socially unintegrated fall into disorder. A former patient wrote that, contrary to my observations, she had never noticed less order in the lives of tuberculosis patients than of other people. But she did add that she has met such patients only in a sanatorium where the head doctor, an affectionate man, had been able to infuse a strong family spirit. In such an orderly atmosphere they were able to overcome their lack of self-discipline, which those who live alone can never do.

Hence, this proud preaching of independence which has

dominated the last three centuries is but folly. Man cannot lay claim to independence, for the sole reason that his life is not his own, that it has been loaned him by his Creator who, according to his own good pleasure, has fixed the laws from which man cannot escape. To God he will have to give an account.

Every independent attitude, every exaggerated individualism, is in the last analysis a revolt against God. This is why we must tell the world, which desires to rediscover the common life, that it will never make this discovery unless and until it first rediscovers the presence of God and kneels down before him. We do not lack for modern prophets seeking to restore a basis of unity for mankind, all on purely human grounds. I would not presume to criticize these men. However, why don't they go right to the inevitable conclusions inherent in their thought? A common life is impossible except by faith. Thus, Bonald made the remark that, in order for men to unite together, they need a basis of unity that is beyond them. More is needed than a common program, which they can choose together and later on dispute. Men need to see more than a social contract in their marriage, their trade, and their state, for a social contract can be as freely broken as made.

Everyone agrees in principle that the world should be united in love, justice, and mutual good will. Everyone claims this for his neighbor. What makes this difficult in practice is, call it what you will, sin. Society will not be reconstructed by a too-easy optimism or by fine juridical laws. To attempt it in this way would be to minimize our universal selfishness, which cannot be broken except by our submission to God.

I am in the act of writing this book when into my study walks my wife, all upset by something. In spite of all that I have just written about the meaning of fellowship, my first reaction is that of irritation. Inwardly, I demand respect for my work, consideration that is due to a writer as he laboriously seeks to express his thought! It is only as before God this first reaction is overcome, and I repent of it as of a sin, that I realize that I can do more for the restoration of fellowship by welcoming my wife joyfully, by sharing my concern with her, and by helping her to accept it, than by closing the door so as to write in peace.

We can discuss faith endlessly, but in practice no one receives faith without an act of surrender to God. The signature upon such an act is always realized by obedience to a specific moral command or by agreement with another human will, against which we have obstinately fought up until now.

However, to surrender this way in the presence of God is not to let ourselves be dominated by those to whom we give in; it is rather to enter a real independence at the very time that we renounce independence as a right. The only way to be really independent of the opinions, criticisms, and demands of others is to put oneself into dependence upon God.

The man who fights with everyone in order to defend his independence is not free at all, whereas the man who has surrendered his life to God and who, therefore, brings a spirit of self-sacrifice into his family and social relationships, possesses this independence that forever eludes the former.

There is no other power capable of breaking the self-will of men, which is the source of all social conflict. God alone can do it, as his grace possesses the soul who receives him as absolute master.

A patient of mine whose life was formerly poisoned by his spirit of independence wrote to me before his appointment, asking that we begin it with prayer. He feared that otherwise the devil would soon change the interview into a sort of hide-and-go-seek.

He who has thus surrendered his life to Christ brings peace into his human relationships and creates a spirit of fellowship. We see it in the army, where just one person in a rebellious spirit is enough to poison the whole unit's spirit, but where also a man filled with the spirit of self-sacrifice is enough to restore a feeling of oneness.

Here is a couple in conflict. The husband is waging a kind of war of nerves, which drives his wife into reactions of tension, depression, and despair that will end up by bringing what he wants, her consent to divorce. She well sees that only God's grace and daily communion with him can make her invulnerable to such provocation and maintain her serenity in the midst of storm.

Yet the Christian attitude is not always to accept all difficulties. A girl was wearing herself out working in a hostile environment where traps were always being laid for her. I reminded her of Christ's words: " If they don't receive you, shake off the dust from your feet " (Luke 10:10-11). Because they are not free from fear of the future, because they are afraid of losing their jobs, many men appear to accept calmly all kinds of injustice all the while cherishing in their heart a sterile revolt. Their attitude is the opposite of self-sacrifice, which is creative and which has love for its motive instead of fear. A colleague confided in me: " My wife couldn't have children, and both of us were quite bitter about it. Then we adopted a child, and the three of us are very happy. Now, if I understand you," he added, " when you subscribe to the theory of Christian surrender, you would disapprove of our decision and would have encouraged us rather to accept sterility as God's will for us? " You can guess with what haste I corrected my friend! It was in their mutual love, in the very spirit of the gospel, then, that this couple received a creative inspiration that was free from any spirit of revolt. This is the spirit of action that characterizes the Christian life. Also, the spirit in which a couple adopts is all-important to achieve success in such a delicate relationship.

Thus fear is the deepest origin of the conflicts that divide men. Dr. Lucien Bovet, in his opening lecture in Lausanne, showed that faith is the only answer to man's anguish. Organic medicine can correct the physical deficiency which at the moment favors the outburst of anguish; psychotherapeutic medicine can free the soul of the past's memories, which eat upon it. But Dr. Bovet added: " The uncertainty of the future is the specific pathological agent which we must face. How can we remove from that which by definition is uncertain and impenetrable the very characteristic of uncertainty and impenetrability? This is as impossible by strict logic as the squaring of the circle. This completely eludes the effect of all our physical, chemical, and psychological therapy. Here is where science ends and faith begins. . . . Anguish is born of fear, and fear of knowledge. The history of human anguish began at the foot of the tree of knowledge." Dr. Bovet concluded, " Total and naïve surrender to the will of Almighty God, sole master of our tomorrows — that is faith, ' the conviction of things not seen.' "

In the history of our nation, one godly man did more than anyone else to help our people realize our distinctive existence and unity and rediscover the sense of community so badly shattered by civil war. That man was Nicolas de Flue, who wrote to the Senate meeting in Bern, " Obedience is the highest honor in heaven or on earth. Apply yourselves therefore to the obeying of one another."

IV

One of the greatest social factors of the past half century, one that has helped place society's problem in an altogether new light, is the emancipation of the modern woman. It is clear that the family group can never again be constituted in its patriarchal form of a few decades ago. The wife, the daughter, the sister, were then completely under the authority of, and dependent upon, the father. Now, on the other hand, the presence of large numbers of women living alone, spinsters and divorcees, contributes greatly to the social break-up whose dangers we are examining. More than any other, modern woman is in complete emotional and moral confusion because of her sudden emancipation. She suffers deeply in her confusion, and spreads it all around. I cannot pretend to deal with the various aspects of this immense problem which our modern world has been unable to solve. My role as a doctor is to utilize certain conclusions drawn from my daily practice.

I approach this question in the light of the drive for independence that has engulfed us as a storm. The two problems are intimately related. After the declaration of the individual's independence came that of the woman's independence, and her struggle for independence ended in total victory. How is she now going to profit from her victory? It seems to me that this is her big question. Will she become intoxicated with independence, or will she bring to mankind a new quality of group experience? Sometimes the victors are victims of their own success.

Victors are often completely surprised and embarrassed with victory: " Today we can see the wife going to the factory in order to feed the family, while the husband is condemned to unemployment because of competitive wages and to looking after the children and keeping the house," writes Elisabeth Huguenin in *Mission de la femme*. " How many distinguished women there are," she adds, "who have won their university diplomas, won a situation of material independence and an enviable social recognition, who are forced to admit that they lack what they really need and that have not achieved their real calling! "

Woman, having taken the man's independence as a model, has affirmed her own independence by behaving just like him. The feminist crusade was led in the name of equal justice — it is not just that men should enjoy rights and liberties denied to women. Thus nature itself was denied, since in any living organism nature differentiates its functions to make them complementary and interdependent. "If woman wants to imitate man," writes Dr. Théo Bovet, " she denies her own mission."

We cannot take woman's mission to be simply that of motherhood, since many do not marry, and many have no children. Before mentioning the unmarried women, I want to point out that the doctor, as confidant of many wives and mothers, knows that their emancipation has brought upon them, too, certain difficult problems.

First, there is the financial emancipation — many married women lived, before their marriage, in complete financial independence. They earned enough to pay a reasonable boarding fee to their parents and to keep twenty-five dollars or more per week for clothes and personal expenses. He who pays the piper calls the tune! The daughter who pays her board can make demands upon parents as suppliers and can become quite free from their authority. They no longer have anything to tell her, since she no longer costs them anything. Moreover, she becomes accustomed to the luxuries of life: expensive clothes, shows, beautiful trips, and sports. These women, once married, find it difficult to put up with quite different conditions. Often the groom earns little more than his bride used to, and it becomes a real problem to work out a budget wherein all the resources are absorbed by the simple necessities of life. Then, too, it is a great humiliation for a woman who was used to spending her money freely to have to ask her husband for the smallest sum of money in order to buy herself a pair of stockings or a book. In the joy of courtship, she had quite sincerely been ready to accept any necessary restriction in exchange for the happiness of love. But in the daily life of marriage, when she has continually to ask for money, when these demands arouse disputes or when they throw cold water upon the marital relationship, when the wife brings criticism upon her spending and no longer feels understood, she begins to wonder if she is really loved, and it may appear to her that she has given up a real thing for a shadow.

Husbands, on the other hand, prove to be extremely sensitive whenever money is discussed. Their wives cannot understand why. For example, if the wife proposes a certain money-saving, the husband gets angry as though he were being reproached. By instinct, man wants to spoil his wife and to provide the finest situation for her. It is because of this that whenever there is mention of financial difficulties the husband exteriorizes his own self-reproach through arguments. He is not able to offer his wife everything that a Prince Charming could give. A couple stops in front of a store window. In complete innocence the wife exclaims, " My, what a pretty dress! " But the husband takes this spontaneous remark as a complaint, for he is far more desirous than his wife that she have fine clothes.

Many women foresee these difficulties and keep their professional career. They do it to make the family budget so much more complete, or more especially to maintain a degree of financial independence and to avoid having to give an account of their personal expenses. Of course, in many poorer families the woman is obliged by necessity to go out to work. Unfortunately, this situation contributes to the ruin of the spirit of oneness in the family. Yet, it is common today to see a woman keep her work and income even in situations where her husband's profession could easily assure the family budget. In this way, each becomes accustomed to a more luxurious life, and the extra earnings are absorbed by whims and pleasures that often they indulge in alone and that only separate them more.

Often the added security that the wife's earnings bring destroys the husband's sense of responsibility as head of the house, and he adopts an attitude of resignation.

Here is an active and intelligent woman who married a very pleasant man who, like many of his kind, was a bit weak-willed and listless. Not long before the marriage she began working in her father's business, where her husband began to work too. She took on more and more responsibility there, but her husband, born with a quite different temperament, was not at all at ease. He became involved in various dealings outside the company, which took up more of his money than they returned. Thus each of them steadily is growing apart from the other. The wife is quite taken up by her work, is in fact therefore dependent upon her father, and works with him. Husband and wife live in the father's house and share their meals with him. Even on Sundays they go out for a ride with him. She has not followed the gospel ruling, "A man shall leave his father and mother and be joined to his wife, and the two shall become one" (Matt. 19:5).

They really do not have a home, and the husband avoids his wife's company more and more because her professional income and steady advancement increasingly aggravate his feeling of inferiority. He hides his failures from her, and when she discovers them he tries to reassure her with promises and half-lies that only widen the gulf between them.

Other wives, who remain at home, achieve similar results by camouflaging personal expenses in the household accounts. "After all," they would say, "since I'm careful enough to save money, it's only right that I should benefit from it and not bother my husband with requests for personal purchases that he doesn't understand anyway." But marital fellowship is dissipated by such little secrets.

Then there is woman's intellectual and spiritual emancipation. Here is a woman who had an interesting professional work before her marriage. She had gone to college and had been active in learned circles. She had musical talent and lived a fascinating and worldly life. She married a small-business man whose whole world was his commerce. Her life now, taken up with the housework and with helping out her husband in his store, seems very tasteless. The troubles she shows appear to me quite simply as an expression of the great disappointment that is eating away inside her and that she does not dare to tell her husband for fear of hurting him. It is always very trying for a couple when the wife is morally and intellectually superior to her husband. The husband, embarrassed and humiliated in her presence, withdraws into himself and seeks out his less educated " chums," who she feels have a bad influence on him. The situation is even worse when the wife, quite erroneously, believes herself superior. This happens often, because of the feminine aptitude in acquiring a superficial façade of culture. I shall return to this subject later. I could mention the great problems that arise when the wife has continued in her career, especially if it is an independent profession such as medicine, law, theology, or commerce. There is a very ticklish conflict between her duties as mother and wife and the duties of her profession. Even where a couple share the same profession, this is more often an obstacle between them than a unifying factor. Only a real and spiritual communion can enable them to avoid this danger.

Finally, there is romantic independence. The young lady used to be jealously kept in a naïve ignorance of the problems of sex. She was told only that a wife must never refuse her husband anything. Today she is fully instructed from her youth up. She claims as much right as the young man to have her own experiences. When she marries, her husband finds in her a woman who thinks of her love life as one of the essential prerogatives of her independence, which she alone is to control.

I could report here numerous examples of moral and psychological catastrophe brought about by the premature and exaggerated teaching of the modern girl in the mysteries of sex. Starting with the idea that the modern girl, called to fulfill a professional career, must not be ignorant and prudish like the country girl of old, instruction is sometimes given with a brutal realism that completely overlooks the woman's inborn need for modesty and refinement. This is intended to eliminate the repression of sex, but the result is the very opposite. The result is women who are disgusted with sex in advance and who know both too much and too little. So excessive sexual instruction is as dangerous as the former lack of instruction. Everything depends upon the attitude in which it is given. Theoretical knowledge in these matters, which is not accompanied by the impulse of the heart aroused by the worthy love of a husband, only creates confusion in the woman's soul. She becomes incoherent and unnatural. Recently I lectured in a girls' high school, after which many came to talk with me in private. What struck me most was that their questions betrayed this incoherence. These girls were instructed in too realistic a way on certain matters while at the same time they were left in complete ignorance on others.

There is another problem resulting from the romantic emancipation of the modern woman. I have been consulted by ever so many fiancées who are the prey of deep inner doubt because they wonder continually if they are really in love with their betrothed. Especially where there is a prolonged engagement are they seen to break up and make up again continually. Soon they are completely bewildered as to their heart's desire, and drive their fiancé to despair. He cannot understand any of this, and finding his fiancée too complicated he leaves her for another woman who is clearly her inferior.

It has always seemed to me that these painful confusions come from a misunderstanding of the specific quality of romantic psychology natural to each of the sexes. The ideal of woman's emancipation is guilty of this. Nature has willed love to be aggressive in the man and passive in the woman. No one can change that. Love in the man needs to conquer and therefore needs to know what it desires in order to assert itself. On the other hand, romantic literature has abundantly illustrated the paradoxical truth that in the woman's soul there is something that impels her to refuse that which she desires: she says no to the man all the while seeking to be conquered in spite of her refusal. Normally, her refusal raises the man's desire to conquer. When, on the contrary, he stops and timidly withdraws into the unhappy and idealistic love of the poets, there is a conflict in him between this passivity and his masculine instinct to conquer. It is eclipsed but never choked off, and he falls into a neurosis.

Thus when a man tells me he wonders whether he loves his fiancée enough to marry her, I have to tell him that it certainly is not the case. If he loved her with a masculine love, there would be no question in his mind.

However, when a young woman comes to see me in this frame of mind, I have to speak very differently, for love in the woman is before all else the disturbing emotion of being chosen, of feeling herself to be admired and desired. If, instead of giving in instinctively to this emotion and surrendering to the caresses of the man who loves her and who would awaken her to love, she analyzes herself and wonders if she truly does love him or not, she is asking herself a man's question, and therefore there can be no answer for her. She simply sinks farther into the morass of her confusion.

I can think of a young couple who came to see me shortly before their marriage, so mixed up emotionally that they were on the point of breaking up. The young lady was the very image of the emancipated woman used to making clear-cut decisions in all matters according to her inner conviction. In the face of her confusion her fiancé gave up his male role as conqueror, out of respect for his beloved's right to free choice. They were both Christians, so it was not too difficult to persuade them that they were led astray by an erroneous philosophy of our day and that they were departing from the gospel, which is in perfect agreement with the demands of nature. " Wives, be subject to your husbands." (Eph. 5:22.)

Recently I saw this couple again, serenely happy and no longer doubting their mutual love. The husband said, " I have learned to be a man," and the wife added, " and I to be a woman."

I know that this recalling of the gospel teaching will offend some of my women readers, who even sometimes ask the pastor to eliminate it from the marriage ceremony. They are victims of the demand for unlimited independence, which has been preached to them. They become its victims in their marital life and come in the midst of their conflict to tell me: " I am disgusted with my husband, who is a child and not a man. He is so hesitating that I have to make the decisions. He contents himself passively with his minor interests and leaves all the responsibilities to me. If only I had a husband that I could lean upon! But he's not a husband! "

Dr. Axel Munthe has written that "women, though they seem unconscious of it themselves, much prefer to obey than to be obeyed. . . ." And later on, when a young colonel said to him, " You're mistaken, my friend, nobody likes to obey; everyone likes to give orders," the same writer replied, " I disagree; most people and almost all women like to obey."

From the despair of not finding in their husband the master that they instinctively need, so many wives become domineering.

If there are so many women who call upon the psychiatrist or the priest to exercise authority over them and to direct them in life, it is in order to make up for the marital authority that the spirit of our age has taught them to resist.

It goes without saying that I am not advocating the wife's passive dependence upon a tyrant husband, but a truly organic unity wherein, in the bonds of mutual trust, each fulfills that function which God has assigned to him or her.

As we saw with respect to the factory, in the preceding chapter, we find again in the case of the family three possibilities: absolute authority for the husband, absolute equality and independence for each marital partner, or a harmonious and organic mutual complementing.

I have just mentioned the great number of confused and ill-adapted women who have to seek the doctor's help. Roughly speaking, there are twice as many women who come to me than there are men, and I think my colleagues find the same situation true for them. I believe this is because women are more fragile than men. Yet, they endure suffering much better than men do. Their fragility lies in their greater felt need of belonging and in the moral and social conditions of our time — this climate of independence that we have discussed, which plunges them into confusion.

Both physically and psychologically, woman's social status has changed more profoundly and more quickly than man's — so much so that she has not been able to adapt to it, and she pays the price in her health. It has led to an abuse of sports, to an overexertion in career as well as a sexual imbalance, and to the cocktail parties as well as to an insatiable changeableness.

If this is true of married women, it is even more true of single women, who have become so numerous today. Carried away by the modern quest for self-sufficiency and independence, they present all kinds of nervous and functional disorders that can be named what you will — today's name for it is neurosis, which tells no more than yesterday's or tomorrow's name. The names are only expressions of inner turmoil. Neurotic ailments break out whenever the soul is torn apart by conflicting forces. In women, there is an unrootable tendency toward submission, self-giving, and love. Yet our era inspires her toward self-sufficiency, self-direction, and insubmission. Caught between these two currents, she is sick.

Here for example is a spinster in her thirties. She lives with her parents. She is sensitive. She greatly needs affection, which she does not find in the atmosphere of her modern family. Her parents do not understand each other. Her father drives himself in his work; her mother finds refuge in daydreaming. All the women of her age earn their own living. She has remained dependent upon her parents without finding any sense of oneness with them, and she feels left out. Two tendencies are in conflict: first, her need to draw closer to her parents, and second, her need to leave them " to live her own life," as we say today. She is not able to decide between these choices; hence her sickness. Her neurotic sickness shames and irritates her parents so that the daughter feels even more estranged and at the same time more dependent and incapable of deciding her course of action. The parents are equally ambivalent, caught between their desire to protect their sick daughter and their desire to reject her as dishonoring them. When she suggests leaving them, they say that they will not hold her back, but in a tone that betrays both their anxiety at letting her go and their weariness from having her.

As the reader suspects, I could enumerate many examples of this situation, with slight variations in factors involved. Here is another spinster, completely under her parents' domination, which pampering has made her frail. They have always told her that she wouldn't be healthy enough to marry. This suggestion has produced such inhibitions that she has missed opportunities for marriage and has been kept dependent upon her parents. But her health has been shaken by an inner conflict that marriage would have resolved. It is easy to understand how this soul is torn between the desire to win her independence and the desire to remain sheltered by maternal protection, broken as she is. Her indecision makes her sickness worse.

Here is another woman, whose inner conflict is similar, not in relation to her parents, but to her very close sister, who has married. She can neither leave her nor live with her as she did before the marriage.

A single woman had no existence in her own right, formerly. She lived dependent upon parents, or brother, or perhaps a religious order. I am not suggesting that it was an ideal situation for her development. At least there was no conflict between contradictory tendencies. She found her state of dependence quite natural. It didn't bother her, since it was the same for all women. By suggesting that she win her independence, the modern spirit plunges her into inner chaos just as long as human fellowship on some new basis is not offered her to replace the social framework that has been taken away.

Our age's incoherence brings many other conflicts and desires to women. In the name of living her own life, with its supposed right to independence, she has been told that she has a right to a sexual life, to motherhood, and that only therein can she really fulfill her destiny. Yet, modern society has not entirely rejected the traditional demands for sexual morality. Hence, woman is torn between two contradictory suggestions.

Here is a woman who lives with her elderly father. After her engagement's break-up, she went into a depression and sought out a doctor. The doctor suggested her that it was her sexual frustration that made her sick and that any lover would heal her. So she threw herself into a crude affair that only repulsed her. She was a noble person who could find harmonious sexual life only in that total gift of herself which is possible in marriage. More than ever before she became torn between opposite impulses. Her sickness grew steadily more acute until the day that she went to her pastor to confess her sin. He was able to help her re-establish an inner unity in a life that conforms to her moral ideal.

I am not saying that the world used to be better. However, at least public opinion proposed to all a way of life that conformed to moral law, whereas today women receive so-called enlightened counsel that can only throw them into the worst kind of inner conflict.

In the office! How strong a moral ideal is needed for her to resist the pervading inclination to free love and to the undisguised flirtation of her employers. She can even risk losing her job. The pressure of the situation is tremendous, supported as it is by the whole philosophy of the right to live one's own life and to know what sexual love is.

Inasmuch as the young woman has some ideal in her heart, she is torn between this ideal, which she cannot be rid of, and its denial, toward which she is led. When her boss, led astray by the doctrine that presents such action as legitimate and of no consequence, takes her into his arms and arouses her feelings, the conflict in the soul of the woman reaches the threshold of illness. She is torn between her instinct, which urges her to give herself, and her conscience, which would refuse.

It all comes back upon us. Dr. C. G. Jung emphasized the " social danger which is present in this army of single women who would like to be married, and who disturb the regular marital unions. . . . Married woman have second thoughts about the institution while the single women believe in it totally; they want to be married."

As a doctor who has seen so much of this, I must state that the first victim is the woman — the mistress every bit as much as the wife.

V

Here we touch upon the problem of female celibacy, which once again I must discuss. Let me assure my unmarried readers that I do so with complete respect for their suffering. I have too often been the confidant of secret and agonizing torments to say, as sometimes I am taken to say, "It is quite simple; just accept it!"

No, it is not easy for a woman, for any woman, to accept celibacy. A spiritual miracle is absolutely necessary, without which the supposed acceptance is only chagrin and repression.

When, as it happened recently, a spinster tells me, "Oh! Love has never been a real problem to me," I rather suspect unconscious repression and not true victory. Victory comes only after real combat. In reality, this young woman was at odds with all who were close to her. The "schoolteacher" remarks that others made about her were a sign of her inner frustration.

As long as she is "young, seductive, and sought after," writes Elisabeth Huguenin in *La femme devant son destin*, "a woman does not worry about marriage. . . . Once the thirties have been reached, . . . bit by bit the emptiness and insufficiency of her life impress themselves upon her. . . . She resists growing old and clings to the past."

For so many women it is a source of such anguish, expressed in innumerable moral and physical consequences, that in order to be of help I should like to analyze the main factors a bit more completely.

First, there is a question of self-respect. Many single women have confessed before me that even in the presence of God they feel humiliated for not having been asked in marriage more than for any other reason. This is why those who have been asked emphasize it rather unobtrusively by saying, "I could have married if I had wanted to." If they can add, "several times," they never omit the remark. For the same reason, she who has never been proposed to invents a beautiful romance, quite guilelessly. She convinces herself that a certain young man who was a good chum of hers, or even one whom she rarely saw, had had a special attachment to her, had loved her. Explanations come ready-made to her mind: it was his shyness or else the opposition of his parents that prevented his asking her — or else it was because she was too circumspect and reserved and refused to flirt so openly as certain of her friends.

This latter interpretation, so flattering to the self-respect, brings with it an ever greater stiffness, an affected indifference to femininity itself. Thus a woman who has never once been sought after generally becomes so neglectful of her appearance. Naturally, her chances of marrying are not enhanced. Spiteful reaction.

Secondly, there is an erroneous conception of love that gives the woman a completely unrealistic attitude. Many single women all through their life imagine love to be a romantic adventure just as they conceived of it at sixteen years of age. Or else they see it as quite distinct from marriage. With a woman, the fusion of sex and affection is a longer and more difficult process than is the case with a man. Such a fusion takes place only in the fullness of wedded happiness, and what is more it is achieved only in a minority of married women. Many women who give the appearance of being the most sensual suffer from an inner blockage and unconsciously seek to compensate for it by their provoking appearance. I have often wondered why certain women who are good-looking, and who burn with the desire for a sensual experience, are always unnoticed. Meanwhile, others who don't even think about it cannot go anywhere without being subjected to undisguised advances. It would be presumptuous to suspect of them unconscious desires that the men can sense.

Whatever the case may be, sensual temptation for the unmarried woman develops in its juvenile, imaginative, and lonesome form, quite distinct from love properly so called. This is so for them because of the disconnection between sex and sentiment. What complicates things further are the wrong ideas they form about it because they have no one with whom they can open up. They doubt that they could ever marry or have normal children, since they have given in to impure temptations. These erroneous ideas, like all others that are bound up with affections or fears, are deeply rooted. Often they are sown by well-intentioned books full of misconceptions. Only the

Biblical message of God's forgiveness can free these women of the ideas and make them confident and positive again in their attitudes toward marriage.

What I believe I can maintain, then, is that real sensuality plays no major role in most of the cases in which a woman becomes bitter about her spinsterhood or gives herself to a lover or a fiancé. Simple curiosity, one of woman's worst faults, plays at least as big a part in it! After having heard so much about it, she wants to know at last by experience what sexual life really is. Then there is the equally feminine trait of pity, another of temptation's tools. I could not number the women who have told me how they gave in because of pity for men who poured out to them their marital woes and told how "misunderstood" they were by their wives. Because they sympathize, they want to give a bit of happiness to these men in their misfortune.

Also, pity will often keep a woman in an affair that only brings her deception and remorse. With all her soul she would like to break it off, but such a step appears to her to be uncharitable. She feels that she is ruining both her own life and her lover's; yet she sinks farther into the dilemma until she begins to think of suicide.

Or else, she fears to be once again all alone! Here we come back to this book's main theme. The man who woos her in order to get what he wants declares such a fondness for her that this gives her something very similar to human fellowship. Thus she feels completely incapable of being plunged again into loneliness.

In all this, sensuality plays little part in her decision, though the world at large takes her to have quite vulgarly given in to such a temptation. She considers it the price she has to pay for the luxury of no longer being all alone in life.

VI

Finally, we must add to this the pervading pull of society in our modern age, which I mentioned a while back. There is another way of being alone, which is very difficult — that of not acting the same as one's office or factory friends. It is hard to avoid a feeling of inferiority from the pressure of their mocking remarks, which veil their desire and resentment. Here we meet the second theme of this book, that is, that it is an extremely difficult task to help people individually to live up to their ideals unless there is brought about a general change in society's attitudes at the same time.

A whole current of thought, originating partly from the psychoanalytic school and partly from the pseudoscientific philosophy of a century ago, has propagated ideas that are totally untrue, according to which sexual relations are a natural need, and therefore are indispensable to a woman's physical and mental equilibrium. Of course, these theories are readily spread about by all who are vainly trying to silence their own remorseful conscience. It is true, certainly, that there are many physical and nervous troubles found among those who remain chaste. But what I am affirming here is that their troubles do not come from chastity, but rather from that very idea which has been suggested to them — that chastity is harmful to them. Many of their troubles stem from their remaining halfway between true chastity and immorality, because of the pernicious atmosphere in which they live. They do not allow themselves the vulgar indulgence of their sexual instinct, but because they are carried along by the general attitude of our age, they continually half expose themselves to temptation, throwing themselves thus into inner conflict between contradictory desires.

Some of our atheistic colleagues suggest, as I have mentioned, that those who have remained chaste re-establish inner unity by giving in to their sexual impulses, which are exaggerated in importance. They suggest what they call "sexual experiments." I have always been baffled by the fact that simple honesty does not force these doctors to recognize that by their philosophy they are throwing these women into even graver conflict.

We can propose only one answer that will stand up: Christianity's answer of absolute purity. Everyone knows that it is a lot less tiring and dangerous to stand on top of a wall than it is to hang on to a few jags halfway up.

The Christian answer, contrary to what many think, implies no negative attitude toward either sex or marriage. In the eyes of God, who created marriage, it is perfectly right for a woman to desire to marry and to pour out the desire of her heart in prayer. The other day I reminded a young woman that on the eve of her birthday a child is asked to make a list of the gifts she would like to get. We drew up her " list " together, and I put at the top: " a husband." Then, when we prayed together, I felt like a mail carrier who was delivering the list to the Father, which he awaited, just as parents expect a list from their child.

Several women have asked me if it is right for a Christian to seek a partner through the ads in the paper. I see nothing in the gospel that forbids it. I know several happily married couples, where both are very shy, who met in this way. There is nothing that forbids our faith to see God's hand working through such a procedure.

The Christian answer for both women and men is to surrender their love destiny into the hands of God. " O God, this instinct which thou hast given me — I offer it up in turn to thee. Direct my life according to thy good pleasure and thine infinite wisdom. If thou art pleased to give me a husband, as I so desire, I want to receive one only as from thee. Even then, keep me from using my instinct for other purposes than for what thou dost want — for my own enjoyment rather than for the fulfilling of thy will for me. If it please thee to keep me single, grant me the grace to accept it with all my heart and to know that my life can be happy and beautiful only if it is according to thy will."

There is no inner conflict and no repression of desire in such an attitude of surrender, providing that it is sincere and deep, and an integral part of one's total consecration. There is neither a deceitful denial of one's desire to marry nor any denial of the sexual drive itself; neither is there any tension because of it.

With regard to marriage, we find the same paradox mentioned in section II of this chapter on social integration; that is, that too great a desire defeats its own purpose. In many spinsters the desire to marry becomes so intense and obsessive that they are robbed of their natural charm, ease, and spontaneity whenever they are in the presence of men. Their desire becomes thus their obstacle to marriage. They cannot look at a man, even one who has the least chance of ever marrying them, without thinking of that possibility. They are so troubled by this that the Christian surrender is the first condition they must meet if they are eventually to find a husband. This vicious circle is both paradoxical and tragic. It helps spread the notion of "the chance meeting" so much in vogue today. It gives victims the feeling that the unconcerned have drawn the happy lot of marriage, while those who wanted marriage so much have missed the lucky draw in life's lottery.

Such a philosophy is demoralizing. Let us put in its place faith in the will of God, who entrusts to each the tasks that befit him within the social organism.

Nowhere does the Bible state, as do today's philosophers, that woman's sole destiny is in marriage and motherhood. I would accuse these ideas of having darkened to the point of despair the lives of countless single people. On the contrary, the Bible speaks to us of many unmarried people who fulfilled their destiny and found a true life in fellowship.

Even atheistic psychoanalysts have come to speak of a sublimation, but one must admit that it seems rather tardy and inappropriate in the context of their theories. Thus to consider the single woman's social activity and spiritual consecration as a minor substitution for sexual experience is to give her, a priori, a negative attitude toward her magnificent possibilities of self-fulfillment through her self-giving in a social vocation.

One of my patients, in some personal notes that she lent me to read, considered "sublimation" as the normal route for the "libido," and sexual life as its inferior expression. I would not go so far as that, for such a viewpoint contains a certain negativity of attitude toward sex itself.

For the Christian, sex is of God when it is fulfilled according to his will in marriage; in the same way the "love of one's neighbor" is of God when he calls a woman to serve in celibacy. There is no priority of values between these two pathways of love.

Many object that this Christian solution cannot be proposed to all women. They do not argue that it is not the right answer; they maintain that it is accessible only to an elite. Even Miss Huguenin, in her very brilliant discussion upon this matter in *La femme devant son destin,* seems to hold such a view. It is always easier to consider oneself "not far enough advanced," and thus to take refuge from God's call. Many people we meet reason this way, but in truth they lack the courage to answer the divine call. Their reasoning contains an apparent humility that becomes for them a very subtle trap. Thus they deny the gospel, for it is not the well who need the physician, according to Christ, but the sick.

If many women think the Christian solution cannot be theirs, under the pretext that a certain spiritual development is a prior condition, this is because they are led astray by current philosophies that contrast the common needs of nature with the possibilities of sublimation for an "elite."

The elite of the gospel is not made up of the "advanced," but of poor devils who accept God's grace.

Finally, among the various factors in the anxiety of female celibacy, we must call attention to one that is quite important: the fear of becoming an "old maid." I have often heard single women, still young, mention an older woman and tell me with a horrified expression, "What I fear most is the thought that I might become just like her." I have always felt quite right in assuring them by mentioning another older woman whom no one would ever think of labeling "old maid." Then I add this remark: "It is up to you whether later on you resemble the one or the other."

What is it that sets unmarried women in such striking contrast? Simply self-centeredness on the one hand and self-giving on the other. The self-centered woman, embittered by resentment at her celibate state, has yet farther isolated herself. She has withdrawn into herself, and is more and more preoccupied with herself — with her every illness, with respect given her particular ways, and with her minor pleasures, which become manias. The self-giving woman, resolutely throwing herself into an inspired and outgoing vocation with the impulse of love that her heart needs to express, has found her home and spiritual family in the sick, the lonely, the poor, and the children whom she has met on her way. This has kept her in the reality of fellowship. This has saved her from sliding into selfishness.

Marriage is not just a question of sex. It is also a school for self-forgetting. In the wife and mother, the many sacrifices she has to make for her husband and children break her self-will. The married woman has scarcely any leisure to indulge in her manias and personal comforts. The husband arrives home when he wants to, and yet the dinner must be ready. When he wants to rest, she must be quiet. When he wants to go out, she must accompany him even if she doesn't feel too well. The child cries at night, and even when he sleeps peacefully she keeps a sensitive ear while sleeping lightly. Thus marriage breaks the self-will and the spirit of independence. This is so true that those married women who dominate their families, who impose their will instead of surrendering it, become "old maids" even though married.

I have been able to see how far the spirit of independence can develop in unmarried women, through those who have confided in me what not being married has meant to them. I used to think that no man would want such a woman for a wife, so unready for the everyday sacrifices of married life. I thought that it was her spirit of independence that had kept her single.

Now I see things differently. Independence is the price a woman is ready to pay for the happiness of being married. If she doesn't get her prize, she keeps her money. She hangs on to the independence that she would willingly have sacrificed for marriage and clutches it now as a consolation.

Thus the greatest danger in celibacy lies in this aggravation of one's natural selfishness and self-will.

Dr. Dubois has written: " Often states of psychoneurosis are found in old maids. It is difficult, however, to say what comes from continence, that is, from the nonsatisfaction of natural needs, and what comes from abnormal conditions of life, the moral isolation in which single women live."

If marriage is one school of sacrifice where woman can rediscover life-in-fellowship, she can also learn it in another school — Christ's. The heart of Christian experience consists precisely in such personal surrender. Naturally, it is easier and more often present in marriage, but it is perhaps more fruitful and yet more complete when accomplished by God's grace alone, for then the sacrifice is a greater one. In any case, it is the only way open to the single woman by which to avoid becoming an " old maid."

How difficult this way is! I have come to wonder if it is not necessary for single women to live in their own communities. All doctors know how difficult it is for groups of women to live together, even when they tenderly love one another. We have all observed those homes where mother and daughter, or perhaps two close friends, live at continual cross-purposes, constantly arguing, and yet inseparably linked together in an unbelievable mutual dependence.

Therefore, in order that such a shared life succeed, a spiritual basis is needed so that it will lead to Christian self-surrender rather than to an aggravated self-centeredness. I know of some examples of community life that are very promising for the future. These are the only attempts being made toward a real solution of the great problem of single women in the modern world. The problem must be solved.

IV

The Spirit of Possessiveness

I

There is a third source of division between men that our age has fostered and that is destructive of fellowship among us: greed, avarice, gluttony, the desire to dominate, intolerance — all of which I shall group together under the phrase " the spirit of possessiveness," which indicates the underlying sentiment common to all.

This is so evident to everyone that here again I will refrain from treating the subject systematically in order to express more extensively some of the insights into certain aspects of the problem, which I have gained through my daily work as a doctor.

Of overeating and of overdrinking I have already written elsewhere. Let me take time to mention, however, what is of interest from the point of view of this book, namely, that there are two types of gluttony: the social and the selfish. For example, I can think of a certain army officer whom I knew who was always talking of exquisite meals and organizing them royally. He would even go to the kitchen to prepare a certain sauce of which he knew the secret. Yet in his personal living he was a man of model frugality. His gluttony was the way in which he expressed his sociableness and affection to his guests and to the officers who were under him. At heart it was the very opposite to that self-centered type of overindulgence which makes so many men slaves to themselves. The same is true of many distinguished housewives, who put their whole heart into serving good meals. My own grandmother kept a little booklet in which she recorded all the menus she had served, so as not to offer the same dish twice to any guest.

The same can be said of alcohol and tobacco, which incontestably can serve to create and sustain an atmosphere of fellowship, whereas alcohol, in particular, also can ruin so many families. With its intellectualistic bias, Protestantism has often belittled the effective simplicity of material things to bring about a spirit of fellowship. Christ did not despise such means. He cooked a meal himself for his disciples after the resurrection, and he wed our remembrance of his supreme sacrifice to the eating and drinking of a festive meal in common.

Here, as in everything else, we see that quite contrary to religious formalism good and evil do not reside so much in what we do as in the spirit in which we do it. What is done out of love for God and for our fellows is good. What is done out of selfishness and desire for personal enjoyment is evil.

Here there is a paradox relating to the thirst for pleasure, and the doctor, who observes men daily, can confirm what clear-sighted moralists have always said, namely, that the pursuit of pleasure brings no happiness. Recently, I attended a fellow doctor's lecture on the question of sex. He approached the subject quite carefully from this point of view: it is a universal law that the pursuit of happiness results only in its loss. Thus the gourmet, spoiled by complicated cooking, no longer can appreciate a good simple meal with its natural flavor, and ends up by no longer finding any refinements good enough to satisfy his insatiable taste for food. In the same way the young employee who in his tempestuous zeal seeks the boss's approval only ends by wearing out the boss's patience. Again, the lover who thinks only of the pleasure that awaits him very quickly destroys his own happiness, whereas another who thinks rather of giving pleasure to the one he loves conserves his happiness and keeps his ardor ever renewed. Therein, if I may say so, lies the mechanism within so many marriages, of the self-destruction of love. These marriages have not been kept alive through Christian experience. In courting, the fiancé had only one thought: to make his betrothed happy. Happiness would fill his heart when he felt her happiness at the smallest bit of attention or at a kiss. Then, bit by bit, he began to keep his happiness for himself. His wife's beauty became no longer an unhoped-for gift, but rather a treasure in his possession, like a work of art that he might have acquired. His mind became accustomed to considering his happiness as a right. From then on he took notice in his heart not of his wife's expressions of love to him but of those which she should have given him but failed to give. For she, too, has begun to notice how selfish he has become, and after all, she doesn't exist just to be at his service.

Love is a bond. A line joining two points can be drawn either from left to right or from right to left. As long as love goes out from us toward our wife, as long as we forget ourselves in order to think of her happiness, we ourselves are happy. When love's direction is reversed, its very nature is negated; it withers. And as soon as we are less happy, we think less of how we can make our wife happy and more of what we think we have the right to expect from her.

Ch. Durand-Pallot formulates the law this way: "Your happiness is found in your loved one's happiness."

This is all very common knowledge, and yet it bears repeating because so many couples fall into this vicious circle. I must mention as well that which happens when, from a spiritual experience, one of the partners is suddenly set free from preoccupation with himself. The direction of the current is once again reversed. Love recaptures its spontaneity and freshness and brings happiness again, even when the other partner remains selfish.

I have seen many couples in trouble wherein each partner lists the countless satisfactions that he or she expects from the other. But he no longer has room in his heart for the real meaning of love, which is to procure happiness for the other. Such tragedies are completely hopeless unless the conversion of one partner takes place.

In the technical sense, this is equally true of the sexual problem itself. Every case of impotence in the man and of frigidity in the woman is closely tied with a wrong attitude toward physical love. The person is preoccupied with himself — with his success in sex and with the desired enjoyment. In this attitude there is self-analysis and fear of failure, which is enough to assure failure, and which in turn will bring self-preoccupation and self-pity.

In this way sexual failure brings guilt feelings with regard to the marital partner — terrible feelings of inferiority, which are the cause of neurotic troubles. These troubles in turn produce doubt in oneself and anxiety for success in sex, which spoils the chances for such success. Here is a young wife caught in this vicious circle. She admits to me that she has gone as far as to betray her husband for the sole reason that she hoped in this way to achieve sexual success with a lover, success she needs in order to prove to herself that she is not sick.

On the other hand, the lover who is so captivated by the object of his love, to the point of forgetting all else, of forgetting even his instinctive desire, experiences his sensual pleasure without seeking it, that is, in procuring it for his wife.

Let me speak to the husbands. Many men "make love," as they say, in a completely selfish way. There are marriages that really are not marriages at all, wherein the husband, far from sharing his whole life with his wife, sees in her only a sexual object that he has acquired legally. That is why so many women are told that love is essential for them and that they must commit themselves completely, whereas it is only a side line for men. Or else, going straight to the point and seeking only his own pleasure, the husband ignores his God-given instinct to awaken his partner to love through caresses. He succeeds only in repulsing his wife from sex life, which ends even for him in the loss of all of its spontaneity and meaning. Others commit the same mistake by a strange sort of scrupulous conscience, which they completely lose when they drift into extra-marital experiences after having failed in their own marriage. They speak of the " revelation of what bodily love can be " without realizing that they behave quite differently with their mistress than they ever did in their legitimate relationships with their wife. Once again, the evil is not in the act itself, but in the selfishness of the heart. Sometimes the same situation is true of the wife. We speak of the incompatibility of tempera-ments. To be compatible, one has to love, that is, to seek more to give pleasure than to get it for oneself.

Of course, each partner can read these lines quite selfishly, seeking to spy out the various faults of his mate rather than his own! How many men there are who in seeking sensual satis-faction see it elude them, after which they turn to artificial affectedness, which only repulses them farther.

"People who have had the misfortune of becoming accus-tomed to violent pleasures," wrote Fénelon, " lose the capacity to enjoy moderate pleasures and weary themselves in anxious pursuit of the thrilling." Dr. Missenard refers to those " wealthy owners of harems " in Moslem lands who, " weary of natural pleasures, have been drawn into dissolute living."

"Pleasure can be based on illusion," wrote Chamfort, " but happiness is built upon the truth."

Naturally, I do not claim that the spirit of self-indulgence is of recent birth. Plato wrote long ago, " Men foreign to reason and to virtue, constantly given to banqueting and to like pleas-ures, are carried so it appears toward all that is base, and thus they wander all their life; never have they lifted their eyes to-ward truth nor aspired to it; never have they tasted solid and pure pleasure, but like animals with down-turned eyes, they are drawn toward the earthy and the feast tables, they feed and fatten upon pillage and satisfy their carnal passions; in order to appease their unsatisfied lust, they rush and strike one an-other with their iron horns and their shoes and kill one another, victims of an insatiable greed."

What I am claiming is that our generation has carried this

craze for pleasure to its limits. Formerly, at least the philosophers condemned it. Today, the Freudian school has not hesitated to speak of " the pleasure principle." The vulgarization of this has let loose the instincts as never before, and with their indulgence has brought suffering as never before. Even the ancient protagonist of pleasure, Epicurus, that humble, refined, and delicate man, distinguished between false and true pleasures — true pleasures being those of the mind — so that the morality he taught did not faintly resemble that which our modern paganism has produced.

It is in this self-centered conception of life that the problem of the falling birth rate has originated. Everyone knows that we suffer from the same sickness as does France in this regard. As the magazine *Information Medicale* recently reported, a midwife who was arrested admitted to having brought about three thousand abortions.

" The birth rate," writes Dr. E. Olivier, " is not even the half today of what is was in 1760. . . . The drop in our birth rate illustrates most strikingly the Biblical verdict: he who would save his life will lose it."

In order to maintain our depopulation, there are 20,000 births too few in Switzerland every year. (Translator's note: For forty years previous to the 1950's, the French and Swiss birth rates were too low even to maintain the population. In the few years since this book's publication in French, the birth rate has made a remarkable recovery in both countries.)

It is a grave sign of the lowering moral standards of a nation. In the time of the Roman Empire, the philosopher Musonius Rufus was very much troubled by the diminishing number of children. " The most harmful thing that can happen to the state," said he.

Those women whose nervous disorders seem to stem principally from this arbitrary restriction upon maternity are quite numerous. Here is one, still quite young, who was sterilized for the sole reason that she was living in the tropics in an unfavorable climate for children. Now she is back home and all the ac-

tivities into which I encourage her to enter are only an insufficient compensation.

In others, a bad conscience exists in addition to the psychological complex. A fervent Catholic comes for consultation
about nervous disorders. Their basic cause seems to lie in the
anxiety caused her by her husband's not wanting to have any
children.

There again, fear in its various forms is the main cause of
disobedience to divine law. These fears include the simple fear
of how a child could upset one's comfortable life, as well as fear
of the future's financial situation, often found in well-off families. Someone has pointed out in this regard that it is the families of civil servants that have the lowest birth rate. This dem-
onstrates that a guaranteed salary and an assured pension, far
from healing man of his anxiety, actually by suggestion polarize
his anxieties upon his financial security.

I have also often hit upon the fear of heredity. Here is a
couple who have been in love for twenty years but have never
dared to marry because the man is afraid of having nervous
children. This pusillanimous attitude and violation of natural
desire has of course taken its toll upon the woman in the form
of serious neurotic disturbances.

To be sure, there are certain cases in which I must quite
frankly warn a fiancée of the strong likelihood of hereditary
weaknesses reappearing in any children she might have. Honesty obliges me. Sometimes it is a real spiritual victory when a
woman thus gives up the prospect of having children. However,
much more often the fear of heredity is very much exaggerated
and is more a symptom of neurotic fears of parenthood. In such
persons an act of faith is needed to improve their health and
lead them into a normal life.

We are touching upon the delicate subject of the need for
medical abortion. One day a pregnant woman came to see me
with her husband. Her doctor had definitely recommended that
her pregnancy be terminated for the sake of her health. The
couple were Christians and were wondering if they shouldn't

take a step of faith and keep the baby despite the doctor's advice. Yet they seemed to be speaking with more fear than confidence. So I said to the mother, with tongue in cheek, "We should never pretend we've more faith than we have; if you really believed with a boldness that is ready to face all dangers, you wouldn't even have come to consult me."

Two years later, I saw this sick woman again, bothered with nervous disorders. Following our first consultation and the abortion, her spiritual life had continued to decline and her condition had worsened. I immediately felt responsible for this. My words had been causative through their negative suggestiveness. Doubting her own faith, the woman had lost faith, and with it her health. It was a humbling experience for me, but it became the beginning of spiritual renewal in that home. Recently they have announced the happy birth of a child.

However, there are more subtle factors having to do with the modern evolution of woman's role. Here is a young wife whose several pregnancies have never come to full term, except for the sole child that she bore living and that died shortly afterward. Her husband was again hoping for a child, but she was fearful. When I saw her doctor, he told me immediately, "I think her trouble is basically more psychological than medical. My client is an intellectual for whom her freedom means more than femininity or the maternal instinct. During her pregnancies, she was unable to make the sacrifices she should have for her child's sake. She climbed up and down the stairs as much as ever, in spite of all my orders."

Then I had a conversation with the couple that was possible only because of our common faith and that brought on some sharp reactions from the wife. Nevertheless, through prayer to God about it, she gradually came to recognize that she had not been inwardly reconciled to becoming a mother. She then followed her doctor's directions with exemplary attention when she next became pregnant. Now there are two fine babies that have brought happiness to this couple.

I can recall many cases of neurotic complaints of various

troubles whose real cause stems from the mental separation of the bodily from the spiritual, of physical love from idealistic love, of sex from sentiment. Often, erroneous ideas or religious emphases are responsible for this. One man, as a child, had had a great admiration for the priest who taught him, and for a time he had wanted to become a priest. From then on, celibacy was forever associated in his mind with every concept of sanctification. Later on, through reading books that naïvely try to preserve young people from impurity by sowing in their hearts all kinds of false fears and negative feelings about sex, he developed a complex of impotence. I sent him to a psychoanalyst who, after a few interviews, told me he held no hope for the man's therapy. Thereafter, only through several long interviews did this patient regain the sense of sex as God-given and come to understand that God's plan is precisely to unite the spirit and the flesh in love, instead of opposing them to each other. Thus was he set free.

A married woman, Protestant, had met an evangelist who maintained that it was a sin to have children. As she is easily impressed and very scrupulous in her religion, she experienced a repulsion from sex that brought on nervous troubles in her life.

A doctor cannot help noticing how few persons there are who are straightforward with regard to sex. Many, even among those who do not consider themselves religious but who are influenced by a so-called Christian tradition, believe they are above it all by affecting no interest in the flesh. It is a type of Pharisaism. Open the Bible and see for yourself how far the Bible is from this false modesty. It speaks of sex in a very frank manner. For a doctor, anyone who claims he has no sexual appetite is only a sick man suffering from a blockage of his conscious or subconscious mind. The blockage is betrayed in a thousand ways, such as jealousy or excessive zeal.

Parents lack frankness toward their children as much with regard to religion as with regard to sexual fact. " During all my youth," said one client to me, " I felt that religion and sex for my mother were locked up in the same secret cupboard of modesty, mystery, and shame." Hence the tenacious but erroneous association of ideas found universally between sex and sin. Not sex, but its use outside God's plan, is sin.

Religious people have more trouble than others in soldering together sex and tender affection, because of the guilt feeling they attach to the one and not to the other. The will of God is accomplished precisely in such a welding of the two, and it is disobedience to want to love with an affective but nonconsummated love. True communion with God leads to the total acceptance of sex to the degree that sex is subject to his will.

The error has originated from a false interpretation, as my colleague Dr. Schlemmer has pointed out, of the opposition often expressed in the gospel between flesh and spirit. The flesh mentioned in these passages, $\sigma\acute{\alpha}\rho\xi$, refers to natural man, the tendency toward sin, which is as much of the soul as of the body. Its opposite, spirit, $\pi\nu\epsilon\hat{\upsilon}\mu\alpha$, is the tendency toward God. But flesh in its meaning as body, $\sigma\hat{\omega}\mu\alpha$, is nowhere opposed to spirit. Indeed, it is declared to be the temple of the Holy Spirit.

Thus the feeling of fear so universally aroused by sex, set forth in the work of the psychoanalysts, disappears precisely when we become conscious of the God-givenness of our sexuality. Apart from God, sex is either a taboo that nobody should mention, or else a divinity to which one becomes enslaved. Under God, it becomes the supreme expression of marital love, just as he has willed it, and at the same time it remains something good to which we have not been enslaved. I believe that sex apart from God, that is to say that the experience of intercourse without an accompanying spiritual communion, can never result in the fullness of sexual happiness. Moreover, I believe that it is from the nostalgia for spiritual communion that many men seek passionately, in vain, a compensation in physical love, and become its prisoners.

Durand-Pallot has well described the three attitudes — Libertine, Ascetic, and Christian — each of which is clearly distinguishable from the others.

The mental separation between flesh and spirit is especially serious in that it leads many wives, who suffer simply from a measure of sex inhibition, to consider themselves superior to their husbands and to belittle them because of their fondness for physical pleasure. I could mention many examples of this, for such women readily come to consult a Christian doctor. In fact, their religious fervor is so much the greater because they unconsciously are seeking in religion a compensation for what they lack, and they show as great a zeal for spiritual things as they show a repulsion for the profane tastes of their husbands. Of course, the gap steadily widens between such couples, and such an understanding of the faith constitutes no attraction for the husband.

A former nurse, who has probably never accepted her change from that noble profession to the more modest one of peasant and housewife, looks down upon her husband and is quickly disgusted by his " vulgarity." The latter, hurt by such contempt, only continues farther in his swearing and in flouting his wife's pedantic cleanliness.

Such women, when they can be helped to see the pride they are nourishing in their supposed spiritual superiority, gain a very different victory from that which they aimed at. Religion commands us to love, and love does not mean opposing one's husband, but rather it means seeking to please him. One wife wrote to me of the surprise her husband had when, after our interview, she suggested to him that they go to the station restaurant for a tasty dinner! Her husband had become accustomed to feeling scorned by his pious wife because of the gastronomical way in which he would express his marital love.

We see men and women who never manage to get married because time after time they enter either into purely spiritual relationships or else into purely fleshly relationships. For them it is necessary that in their deepest heart this mental opposition of the two cease if they are ever to know the total self-giving that constitutes marriage. It is only in this way, in marriage, that the fusion of flesh and spirit can take place according to the divine intent. One man, filled with certain psychoanalytic theories, wanted to cure the woman he loved of certain of her " complexes " by leading her into a " sexual experience." However, her liberation is completely negative and brings her no sense of liberation, for she has too high a soul to give herself over to such love without that complete and categorical commitment which exists in marriage. She stays with her lover out of pity for him, and both of them are unhappy even though they both share a mutual love.

For those who do not oppose the union of spirit and flesh, spiritual love awakens and enlivens the physical love, and the latter in turn enriches and strengthens the spiritual bonds. Often we see a couple at odds with each other who sincerely believe that their misunderstanding is from a physical cause. " What can I do about it? " the man says. " You cannot force yourself to love. I used to love my wife, but I'm no longer drawn to her. There's nothing I can do about it." A woman's attraction is undefinable. " It isn't the most beautiful women that are the most desired," wrote Henry Bidou. This is true, and we can add, " Every woman is beautiful when she is loved and when she feels loved." This husband who no longer finds his wife as beautiful as she used to be is probably responsible for her premature aging. A fervent love would have preserved her from it. There is — and this must be stated simply and in spite of all that the poets tell us — a considerable role that suggestion plays in physical love. When a husband begins to tell himself that his wife is no longer beautiful enough for him, he no longer finds her beautiful, and she begins to lose what beauty she has because she is no longer desired. The man tells himself that he needs a young woman, and falls in love with his typist, who is not necessarily a beauty. Quickly he convinces himself that he cannot live without her, that he is " thunderstruck," and that therefore there is nothing he can do to extricate himself.

II

Gluttony of the flesh is not the only kind of gluttony. I have met many spiritual gluttons who, because they've made their intellectual cultivation a source of pleasure, have become sterile and dilettante. Or else, by their search for religious feeling, they see it constantly taken away before their eyes. Certainly, any authentic spiritual experience brings about a flowering of the personality that is quite comparable to that produced by sexual happiness, but it is one of those gifts " added unto you " for the person whose one aim is to obey God. It is refused, however, to the one who seeks it as the goal of his religious life. What a tragic thing it is to see these unquenchable souls passing their life in torment in a kind of hunting expedition for religious experience. This is not to mention those who have known the grace of God in a moment of blessing and who ruin their whole spiritual life afterward trying to reproduce that experience.

I have taken the example of sexual pleasure because it is my task as a doctor to speak on this, but everyone will recognize that I could have easily spoken of any other hunger for possession, especially of that for money. Besides, as Zuckermann has shown it to be true among monkeys, sex is often only a means to gain other personal " advantages."

There is no need to dwell upon the role of greed as a cause of division, social injustice, and dissolution of human fellowship. To mention but one medical example, let me recall that just before the war Professor Lemoine, of Paris, stated that the reason for the " bad bread " being sold was none other than " the profit motive, [which motivated] the sacrifice of quality for speed and quantity in production," and that at every level — the baker, the miller, and the farmer as well.

The story is told of a rabbi visited by a wealthy neurasthenic who told him of his troubles. The rabbi had him stand before a mirror and asked what he saw. " I see myself," replied the man. Then the rabbi led him to a window and asked what he saw. "I see some men," was the reply. "Well," said the rabbi, "do you know what makes the difference between the two sheets of glass? One of them is covered with silver!" (Translator's note: In French, "silver" and "money" are the same word.)

Gustave Thibon has well demonstrated that one of the causes of dissolution in modern society is the fact that alongside the numerous homes where social injustice prevents income from matching expenses, an easy luxury is widespread among many others who lack the moral strength necessary to resist its pernicious influence. He speaks of our age: "Lots of credit available for the nonessentials, . . . while credit for the essentials such as food and clothing has almost completely disappeared." He adds, later on, "True luxury contains an ascetic note."

Plato denounced wealth as the cause of society's decay.

"What you would keep you lose, and what you give you keep forever," writes Dr. Munthe. "Besides, you have no right to keep this money for yourself; it doesn't belong to you. It belongs to the devil, who sits night and day at his counter behind his sacks of gold destined for the traffic in human souls. Don't hold on to the dirty quarters in your hand for too long. Get rid of them as soon as you can, or the cursed silver will soon burn your fingers, poison your blood, blind your eyes, infect your mind, and harden your heart. Put it in the poor box or throw the wretched coins in the closest gutter, for that is their rightful place. Why pile up your money? You will lose it in the end. Death possesses its own key to your vault. . . . Anything truly beautiful is never put up for sale but comes as a gift from the immortal gods. . . . The birds sing to us for nothing. . . . We have the right to pick the wild flowers that surround us as we walk beside the road. There is no admission ticket necessary to walk under the vault of night, resplendent with the stars. The poor man sleeps better than the rich. Simple food tastes better in the long run than that of the Ritz."

My daily experience has shown me that some people quite indifferent to their money are very much enslaved to another cherished possession. For one, it is a garden from which he could never separate; for another, it is his paintings or his library. Many become hopelessly tied up rather than give up a certain way of life, not because they really like it, but because it allows them to keep something they treasure whose power over them they are loathe to admit. For one woman it is the memory of a lost son that has become her religion. She keeps his study just as it was, with all his furniture, which ties her down to her too-large apartment. Here is a patient in the midst of crisis when her daughter is marrying, even though she admires her future son-in-law. I learn that she once attended a very pious sect in which she was very zealous. One day her fellow believers told her that her faith demanded that she give up her luxurious home. But she lacked the courage. Ever since, she has clung to her home, which has become her god and has taken all her energies. She has had no other interest besides keeping it clean and beautifying it further. Now, I don't know if God ever wanted her to sell her home. However, I do know that the disobedience to what she believed to be God's will did break her life and has been the source of inner tension that broke out critically at the moment of another loss, which this time she could not prevent.

The spirit of possession can seek noble objects; it then becomes the sorrowful caricature of something beautiful. Often, for example, we see nurses — sisters of charity — who have chosen their calling out of idealism and, precisely because they are so proud of it, withdraw jealously into themselves. They say "my sick ward" as if it belonged to them. Woe to anyone who would enter this sacred hall, even if it was to render a service, or who would not show sufficient reverence for the authority of the nurse. Likewise, a scholar who has spent himself in specialized research shows all the reactions of having been robbed when a paper on the same subject appears under another signature.

Here are two students. After a spiritual experience, they began to talk freely to one another on deep matters. It was the start of a real friendship, deep, spiritual, and beneficial to both. Later, one of them showed signs of great psychic confusion, and when he began to examine himself before God, he saw that the character of his friendship itself had been a trap to him. It had become possessive, and he could not stand seeing his friend having as close relations with others as with himself. I could give a good number of examples of this kind of friendship which amounts to the monopolizing of one friend by the other and, naturally, brings only suffering to both. They explain it by saying they like each other too much. But that is impossible. I think that their affection is unbalanced. How many couples, too, instead of finding in their love for one another a motivating impulse for affective relationships with those near them, isolate themselves in dyad selfishness. We know what sin is: " all that separates from God and our fellows." If love or friendship, no matter how noble they may be, separate us from others, they are contaminated by sin.

Here is a grandmother who is so possessive of her daughter in her affection that she becomes jealous of her grandchildren! Their mother shows more love to them than to her. In this atmosphere she gets more pain than joy out of family life, and she tells me that she feels her love is even more of a burden to her loved ones than to her.

Jealousy can be even more subtle. Here is an elderly spinster who has had a difficult life. She had an abnormal brother for whom she has nobly given her whole life. In spite of poor health, she had always worked hard and kept him and given him the care he needed. In spite of it all, she was happy, but now that he has died she is inconsolable. She could enjoy a quiet retired life, but now she can no longer put her heart into anything nor give affection to anyone. Obviously, her mourning doesn't explain all her distress. Her sacrifice for her brother was really the great treasure of her life. She was proud of her sacrifice, but now she sees that she has lost it. She even torments herself in self-reproach for not having done more for him, for he might thus have lived longer. This unhealthy remorse is the projection of a too-strong self-love that she had put into her devotedness.

We meet this pride of sacrifice and enjoyment of the noble role quite often. Here is a couple in strife. The husband lists all the concessions he has made to his wife without having been repaid in kind. So I suggest to his wife that she make an important concession, and in a moment of generous outburst she accepts this challenge. But instead of being appreciative, the husband is more irritated than ever; his noble role has, so to speak, been stolen from him!

This is a subtle sin that I have often spotted in myself. That is why I prefer helping others to accepting their help. It is with great difficulty that I let myself be indebted for some kindness, because I am more covetous of others' esteem than of their kindnesses.

Here is a woman brusquely halted in her activity by an incurable sickness that assures only long months of suffering. She took pride in her affection for " her three men " — her husband and two sons. She gave them tireless, devoted service. Now she sees that she will have to learn to express her affection in a new way, by letting them take care of her now.

I have met many mothers who were far more than reasonably devoted to their husband and children, who tirelessly sought appreciation for their zeal and just as tirelessly refused to be released from their numerous tasks. They claimed they couldn't afford to take holidays from home, though their families could very well have gone without them for a while; thus they jealously guarded the precious treasure of self-sacrifice.

This leads me to a consideration of possessive love of parents for their children. Of course a child is a treasure! However, he is only a loaned treasure, and because they forget this, many parents completely spoil their child's training. They also assure great suffering for themselves later on.

" Children belong to God before they belong to parents," said

Roger Vittoz. One of my clients, a teacher, used to write: " Parents, your children are not your playthings. Their life cannot be yours."

Dr. Tina Keller has written, " Mother-love often is selfish," and Dr. G. Liengme goes so far as to say, " Affection for a child . . . can become a cause of mental unbalance." He means unbalance in the father or the mother. However, that will bring unbalance in the child as well. Out of my last few years' work with neurotic patients I have just counted fourteen cases wherein a mother's possessive love apparently was the decisive factor in bringing on psychological troubles in the child.

Some children have been kept away from life and society by their mothers, who were too desirous of protecting them from the dangers of the world. Some children have parents who are very jealous at the slightest indication that anyone else — teacher or parents of friends — is exercising any influence upon their children. Others have been thwarted in their tastes and in their vocational choice because they were forced by their parents to try to succeed in vocations in which their parents had been ambitious but had failed. Here is a mother who wants her daughter to have a good education because she had always regretted not having had one herself. She stops her from going to the ball, not because she doesn't approve of dancing, but because she is afraid that it will interfere with her studies. The daughter thinks far more of social life than of intellectual pursuits.

Here is a grown-up girl who has never been able to receive mail without her mother's reading it. Here is a woman who was once engaged for a year without ever having been alone with her fiancé — not a minute without his mother's being present, right up until the wedding. Here is another mother whose possessive love for her son was so strong that she has been sick ever since his marriage. It is true that in this case the daughter-in-law was obliged to take energetic action in order to pull this son away from his mother. Here we touch upon the tragedy of dominating love: by trying to keep in your possession the loved one, you lose him. Such love is, in fact, a terrible burden. Either the child is crushed by it and only vegetates, withdrawn and neurotic and becoming his mother's despair, or else he openly rebels, to her complete consternation. She cannot understand why he should be so ungrateful. Here is a mother who has just asked me to arrange for a meeting with her son, a man in his forties. She is completely surprised when I answer to the effect that her son is old enough to ask me, if he wants to. His confidence won by this incident, her son comes to see me right away, and I see for myself the extent of the disaster. His mother, who has bitterly suffered from her parents' divorce, entered into life with a desire for revenge, if I may put it that way. First she wrought it upon her husband, until one day he had had enough and left her. Then it was her son whom she despotically dominated, and next the girl who might have become her daughter-in-law but whom she chased away. Then there was her second child, a daughter, long since in a mental hospital. The son's only solution has been to turn to alcohol. This in turn has provided his mother with another reason for dominating him — in order to save him.

Here is a mother who doggedly forces her son to do his homework, even though he is grown up, and in spite of the fact that she has never taken his subjects. It is her compensation for the fact that her husband already had a son from a previous marriage. This son is her property. However, this attitude is self-defeating, for he is not succeeding in school. Yet she pushes him that much harder.

Often, too, a mother's possessive love for her son is in compensation for the failure of her marital life. This is true of many divorced women who " dedicate themselves " to their child and demand his complete dependence, which consoles them of the bitterness left by their husband's defection.

Here was a lad who, upon my questioning, told me of the dream he'd just had: he had stolen an apple in the market, and the saleswoman was running after him in order to take it away.

"Who does the saleswoman look like?" "She looks like my mother." The story is clear. This young man had become friends with a girl of whom he was very fond. Knowing his mother, he felt that if she came to know about this, she would immediately put an end to it.

Think of the parents who expect their children to spend every Sunday with them, even after they are adult and married! Think of those who will not let them travel abroad! They think that in this way they protect their children from life's temptations. All they accomplish is to break in them the moral power needed to withstand temptation. Overprecaution on the part of the parents usually ends up in producing the opposite effect. Those who keep their children indoors for fear of sickness only make them fragile. Those who keep them cooped up for fear of moral dangers only stimulate the desire for immoral adventures. Here is a woman who lived such a childhood and who might well have turned out badly if her conversion to Christ had not cut her adventure short at the most unexpected moment. She is happily married now and realizes that her behavior was a reaction against her mother's domineering and too-close supervision. As fruit of her spiritual experience, this woman has now been able to forgive her mother.

"It is often because of the possessive love for one child that parents refuse to have any others," remarks Mr. Durand-Pallot. "'In order to give him the best . . . we want him to remain alone.' And conversely, an only child easily can call forth a twisted love from the parents: he becomes a 'daddy's boy,' lifted to a social rank to which he cannot hold and where he feels inferior and unhappy." Durand-Pallot adds, "An only child is often raised in a baneful atmosphere, in the fear of what might happen to him."

Children raised under such pressure of possessive love become unsociable: "I'm afraid to weary another with my love," one of them wrote me.

When parents consider their children as property, their faults and even certain quite innocent acts of behavior are taken by the parents as personal affronts. This is why so much punishment is solely the expression of parental wrath.

Many domineering parents have sent me their child at the moment when he was beginning to get away from them and show signs of independence, which they judged as dangerous and outrageous. Such parents are quite convinced that they are motivated only by concern for the welfare of their child. They want me to be their reinforcement, so that they may win the battle between their will and the will of the child who is affirming himself. They are quite sure that a Christian doctor will not fail to preach respectful submission to parental authority. How astonished and disillusioned they are when I seek instead to understand their child and to help him become conscious of his personal aspirations, which for so long have been suppressed. These parents are never interested in anything but their opinion on the welfare of the child and do not know what joys they are missing by their neglect in listening to him in order to discover and learn something new.

There is much public discussion about methods of education: is it good to punish and to exercise a rigorous discipline and demand complete obedience, or on the contrary to allow a great deal of freedom? What many people have told me about their childhood years has convinced me that the method in itself is not very important. Each has its advantages and each its dangers, according to the spirit in which it is applied. It is just this spirit, this quality of love — generous or possessive — which counts.

The worst situation is found when the parents do not agree. The father may think that he must be strict. The mother, in order to balance this excessive severity, spoils her children behind his back. Or else the mother fears for them and the father feels she is overprotecting them, so he sends them off into life pretending that he has no worry about the physical and moral dangers that await them. Or again, the father is opposed to their receiving any money, whereas the mother, feeling sorry for the children, secretly gives them money for whatever desire they may have. Each parent exaggerates his error in order to balance the opposite error of the other. Each is convinced that it is only his desire to apply the best method of pedagogy that guides him, and he takes whatever justifies his point of view from the books or lectures he may find available. Thus each tries to prove the other wrong, neither of them realizing that their difference of principles is really nothing but an exteriorization of marital discord.

The most important thing in the child's upbringing, more important than any methodology no matter how scientific, is the complete unity and accord of the parents. The most they can do for their children is to meet one another again, recognizing that a spirit of contradiction has carried them too far. Then they can be reunited in the mutual attitude: they will both be strict in certain circumstances and very liberal in other circumstances.

Of course, this spirit of domination is found in other relationships besides those of parents and children. Old housemaids can become veritable tyrants over a bachelor whom they judge incapable of doing without them. They make him in effect a dependent of their despotic care.

Here is a woman who shows psychological disturbances each time her husband leaves for military service. Finally, her husband gives up his career to re-enter civilian life. But — when marching orders, which must never be questioned, come to him as a home guardsman and take him out of the possessive grasp of his wife, in spite of all his professions of love by which he tries to reassure her, he feels deep down in his heart like a schoolboy whose summer vacation has arrived. It is that inner joy which his wife feels intuitively and which arouses her jealousy and suspicions.

An element of domination often creeps into good works such as charity, teaching, and even the spiritual ministry. Those who can love only the people whom they consider socially inferior to themselves or about whom they can complain, and those who are always happy to show off their knowledge but never show interest in another unless it is to instruct him, never listening to him — such people imagine themselves to be motivated by love, whereas actually they are driven more or less consciously by the need to dominate. Poor people are not fooled, nor are those who receive the lessons. We can hurt a person by our gift of money and even by our pity.

The same is true of spiritual life. Love always means going to others, not demanding that they come to us. Nothing is more tragic and cruel than the spiritual tyranny we meet so often. He who has had a rich experience wants to impose it upon others, no holds barred, in order to save them. However, he does not realize the infinite variety of ways by one of which each person needs to find freely what he is seeking. He is unaware of the spirit of judgment and pride that permeates his effort at religious instruction and that soon impedes his work.

Does this mean that we cannot help others? Of course not, but we can be of more help in sharing our difficulties with them than in sharing our victories, in bringing out their good points than in analyzing their sins, in understanding them than in trying to set them right. What makes a spiritual ministry difficult is that people come and ask for advice: " What should I do? " Strictly speaking, we can never know, for a religious experience takes place only if the individual obeys an inward call rather than an external precept. I always feel most helpless in the presence of another soul. No technique can suffice unless there is the Spirit's moving, which we cannot control. I am encouraged, nevertheless, when I notice that it is precisely when I feel most useless and powerless that I am sometimes able to help others. Christ acts when man is without hope. In the fellowship of faith we all stand at the same crossroads, but we have come there by different routes. A spiritual ministry does not mean saying to people, " Take the same pathway I took; it's the best one." It means rather following them through all the turns of their twisting pathway with love and patience, never losing hope even when they seem to be going in the wrong direction.

Here is a woman who a few years ago had a wonderful spiritual experience that healed her of a nervous depression. Since then, she has been zealously concerned about her husband, seeking to lead him to the same ideas and practices of faith. Recently, fresh disturbances took place in her that needed the care of a colleague. These disturbances had a spiritual dimension. Now she had come to tell me of her great discovery, made in the course of her therapy. " I suddenly saw how much I considered myself superior to my husband. In my desire to save him, I saw only his faults. Now I see his good points. He has more than I, and I need to realize this."

Without tolerance, there is no true love. Fénelon wrote, "We can always understand those we love if we love them in good faith, and for what they are."

Here is a couple who have already shared fine experiences. In a time of difficulty they opened up to one another in forgiveness and reconciliation. So they think they know each other. Their confidence becomes their trap. The husband interprets his wife's every word, gesture, or reaction in the light of what he thinks he knows of her and in the light of her faults. She feels that he no longer desires to understand. Formerly he would look at her as if to solve a thrilling mystery, but no more now. She feels judged but not loved. She returns the same to her husband in her behavior. They are that much more despairing now that they feel themselves so far from each other, because they once knew what real fellowship is.

Once one has discovered a fault in his mate, he looks for its reappearance constantly, which registers as so many confirmations of his judgment. It annoys him increasingly, and this hinders the other from improving, all of which only embitters his rejecting and critical spirit. His attitude stops him from seeing that inner tragedy taking place in his mate which is the origin of his mate's visible fault. Only by seeing the inner debate going on in another person is one able to be set free from a critical spirit. We can understand people only when we are free from every preconceived idea about them.

Most couples who differ much in character have great difficulty in understanding each other. Yet, the most thrilling thing in life lies in this difference. Here is a husband, reasoning, logical, realistic. His wife is intuitive, full of imagination, poetic. Starting from his point of view, the husband takes his wife's traits to be so much useless nonsense and tries in vain to prove it to her. How much richer he would be if he would learn from her what is missing in him. " I didn't continue that discussion," wrote such a woman in her diary, " because I have only intuitions to reply to F's reasoning. I am at a disadvantage. I am certain that I am nearer than he to real life, but how can I lead him to share my feelings? " In our rational civilization, such people are always pushed down. Yet we need them so much. My own wife knows this — she who one day when we came to understand each other told me, " I ended up by keeping quiet, because you always had the last word with your reasonings that showed me to be wrong."

The sensitive say they are always pushed down. Thus they express their deep need of meeting others humble enough to be able to listen.

III

For this reason, Christianity rejects the spirit of possession and domination in favor of its unbelievable message of self-surrender and love. In the name of the One who poured himself out, it demands an absolute self-renunciation. There is no other possible fount for a renewal of the meaning of fellowship in our world.

Father Raymond tells the charming story of a little child whose mother was teaching him to pray. When he got to the part, " Lord, I surrender everything to thee, everything I own," he abruptly broke off and whispered to himself, " except my baby rabbit."

All of us have our baby rabbits. Sometimes it is an ugly thing, sometimes beautiful, sometimes large, sometimes small; but we are more attached to it than to anything else. But this is the thing that God asks of us and that he touches upon when we sincerely ask guidance of him. God does not, however, ask us to seek out our neighbor's little rabbits. Those who are greedy only in spirit condemn the love of money in others, and those who thirst only for glory condemn the base sensualism of the gay set.

No one, apart from Christ and the early Christians, has expressed and lived out in a more striking manner this self-deprivation and this love than did Francis of Assisi and his band of the first Friars Minor. " After the Lord had given me some brothers," Paul Sabatier quotes him, " no one showed me what I must do, but the Most High himself revealed what I ought to do, according to the rule of the holy gospel. . . . Those who presented themselves in order to embrace such a life gave to the poor all that they had. They contented themselves with but one tunic, to which they could add pieces to either side. We also had rope and breaches, but besides that we wanted nothing. . . . We loved to stay in poor and abandoned churches and we were simple men, serving all men." Social concern, not just individual salvation, was very present in Francis' soul. He both began and ended his career by re-establishing peace in his strife-torn home town.

Self-renunciation was never an end for Francis as it is for so many whom we see impose upon themselves ascetic exercises for their soul's salvation. It sprang forth from his matchless love: his love for God, his love for nature, and his love for men, among whom he always had a special fondness for lepers and tramps.

" For long I had thought that self-renunciation was the highest expression of the soul," I read in the personal diary of an outstanding woman. " Now, however, I know that it is love that truly gives length, breadth, and depth to the soul, and that self-renunciation has meaning only when it is an outworking of a great love."

Many of our people are confused in this way, to the point

where they cannot imagine God's will as ever coinciding with their desires or tastes.

It nevertheless remains true that real love is disinterested. Listen to the deep confession of one of my patients who told of her life: " I loved love itself more than my lover."

Yet it has to be said — and this shows to what extent love evades all analysis — that neither do we want a love so disinterested that it seems like an " act of charity." " What disturbs me," wrote one wife, " is that I cannot do without my husband, whereas I feel he could get along without me. His love is an act of generosity toward me. But I want to feel that he really needs me." The truth is that the husband probably needed his wife much more than his masculine pride would permit him to let on.

In the second place, real love is spontaneous. I can think of a woman who told me that she accepted her husband as she would a cross, and that her pity obliged her to bear her cross faithfully. She imagined herself to be motivated by Christian love. I would think her husband was scarcely moved by such a love and probably did not even feel himself to be loved.

" To change the attitude of the one who has fallen," wrote Dr. Dubois, " it is not enough to consider the unfortunate circumstances of his life, or to show him sympathy. He must be loved as a brother, lifted up by the arm in the deep realization of our common weakness."

The above writer did not consider himself a Christian, but he surely was one. He proved in a remarkable way the deep relationship between love and humility. Unless they feel as brothers in misery toward those they help, the social worker, doctor, nurse, and pastor will quickly slip down into a forced and condescending love that is the result of a sense of duty.

Often I have surprised myself by pretending to care for a patient more than I really did, by assuring him with kind words that were more from habit than from the heart or that were even supposed to hide a certain hostility aroused in me by some characteristics in the patient. There is no need to emphasize that such love accomplishes little. Yet, miracles are wrought when one confesses his lack of love and humbles himself for it.

The gospel says, "Thou shalt love thy neighbor," not "You must love him." Love born of duty is not yet real love. It can, however, lead to it. "Thou shalt love" is a proclamation of faith. If we lack love, we cannot pretend to have it, nor force ourselves into it. All we can do is to ask it of God, believing that he will give it to us. Well do I remember the day when I realized that my social career and even my religious activity had its roots much more in zeal for a cause than in real love for my fellows.

"Love for medicine is impossible without love for fellow men," wrote Hippocrates. Dr. Lieck spoke of "the pastor of a remote and poverty-stricken area in Estonia, . . . where the main cause of its uplift was the deep interest and love shown these poor people by their pastor." They came in crowds to hear him and to speak with him.

Thirdly, true love is pure. A sick woman, greatly distressed, sought help from a minister. The latter was seized with pity for her. And so, carried away by sympathy, they slid unconsciously into the sinful road to impurity. Instead of being humbled by this fall, the minister justified himself to her by giving complicated theories in which carnal and Christian loves are confused. These theories, even more than the sin, became for her a terrible obstacle to faith.

We need to remain on our guard. There always remains something of the prince charming in a man's instinct, seeking to awaken the sleeping beauty. The hero is easily trapped by the one he saves from a terrible fate. Into the finest spiritual ministry such a feeling can enter, almost imperceptibly. Under the conscious cover of the noble effort of saving another there slips unconsciously an element of desire and enjoyment.

Love can be spoiled by impurity, even between man and wife, when a man desires his own wife at a time when God does not will it.

Once again, this is not to say that the Christian attitude is negative toward physical love, as many erroneously think. To the contrary, this is one of the most amazing gifts we have from the Creator. "Like the feeling of hunger," writes Weatherhead, "the sex instinct is a natural desire, and both of them are part of God's plan."

As in all things, the Christian attitude means to seek God's will in the matter of sex. It means neither the submission to an imposed moral code nor self-abandonment to the unchecked life of immorality. Even between man and wife God's will can be sought! The mutual seeking of God's direction, day after day, for their sexual life, is one of the highest expressions of their love, their reciprocal trust, and their surrender of self-will. This will lead them at times to practice physical love without any false guilt feelings, and at other times to live in chastity without any repression, that is, to "spiritualize their sexuality," according to Dr. R. Biot's fine expression.

Love is not just some great abstract idea or feeling. There are some people with such a lofty conception of love that they never succeed in expressing it in the simple kindnesses of ordinary life. They dream of heroic devotion and self-sacrifice. But, waiting for the opportunity that never comes, they make themselves very unlikeable to those near them and never sense their neighbors' need for affection.

To love is to will the good for another. Love may mean writing with enough care so that our correspondent can read without spending time deciphering; that is, it may mean taking the time to save his time. To love is to pay one's bills; it is to keep things in order so that the wife's work will be made easier. It means arriving somewhere on time; it means giving your full attention to the one who is talking to you. To miss what he says means that we are more interested in what we are telling ourselves inwardly than in what he is telling us. To love is to try to speak in his language, even if we have mastered it but poorly, rather than to force him to speak ours.

This principle is true figuratively as well. Here was a woman in love with spiritual things. She longed for communion with her husband, that is, communion such as in elevating conversation. The husband, a mundane and down-to-earth soul, expressed his love for her, rather, by fixing her kitchen and furniture. His wife, instead of hugging him, would complain that his fixing dirtied everything. She wanted him to speak love to her in her language, and she could not hear him when he spoke thus to her in his own.

To love is to give one's time. We never give the impression that we care when we are in a hurry. Too many social and pastoral counselors are people in a hurry. Hence, people admire their devotion and doubt their love. I am ever struck by the tranquillity in which Christ walked along, always having time to speak with a poor woman beside a well, or replying to the stupid questions of his disciples the very eve of his Passion. To exercise a spiritual ministry means to take time. If we want to save our time for more important matters than a soul, we are but tradesmen. A colleague once said to me, "I don't understand how you find patience to listen to these interminable stories without any interest which people force upon us." If he only knew how it becomes interesting, once we become interested in people!

Regarding time, let me mention a word about the great diversity in the rhythm of life of people. A man may have a quick and prompt temperament, while his wife has the very opposite. Thus she never is able to make a decision, because her husband never gives her the time. Some people, in the first interview, express all their central anxieties to the doctor. Others, however, open up only if favored by a very special atmosphere, which may present itself rarely.

Therefore, let me express the deepest meaning of what I'm trying to say here by what was said of the parliamentary spirit. What is lacking in our hurried, formal, and shallow civilization is love.

"Love is the very essence of Christian fellowship," writes Edouard Burnier.

V

The Spirit of Just Demands

I

All of this will become clearer if we examine now the fourth specific quality of our modern mind which helps weaken human community. This is the universal spirit of rebellion, of self-assertion, of criticism, of demands and jealousy, which abounds today.

"There are so many pieces that go together to make up this world's happiness," said Bossuet, "that there are always a few missing." Hence, simply by encouraging people to consider what they are missing rather than the privileges which they are enjoying, we can stir up a tremendous tide of claims and complaints. Nothing is more contagious than such a spirit. To the doctor this is a real endemic disease.

The poor man envies the rich man for his money and comfort, while the rich man envies the carefree life he has lost. The spinster envies the married woman, and the childless woman envies the one who has the joy of motherhood; we even see some with a few children who want more, so much so that they become sick, while others complain unendingly about the worries and the work that their large family demands of them. Each thinks that the other's life is easier than his own. Thus the spinster has the idea that married women have been able to fulfill themselves easily. Well, it is easy to be married, but not to fulfill oneself in marriage. It is equally difficult for everyone — men, women, single, or married, to fulfill themselves, that is to say, to forget themselves and to give themselves.

Sick people rebel at having to suffer, while others are well who deserve health no more than the former deserve sickness.

" Our fever for equality," writes Gustave Thibon, " is one of the deepest and most serious ills of our age. . . . In the end, nobody finds himself able to stand being unequal to anyone else in anything."

Look at the papers and you will see nothing but demands: producers' demands, consumers' demands, civil servants' demands; women's and businessmen's demands against the trusts, and the trusts' demands against any measures taken against themselves. We complain of the rising cost of living, of the weather, and of the sleep we lose. I read the other day this little dialogue in the humor section of a newspaper:

" Do you remember when we could buy a hen for fifty cents? "

" You used to buy them often? "

" No, never — I found they cost too much at that time."

Men who believe themselves noble-minded waste their lives in protesting against everything, in correcting everyone, in writing scorching letters, in sowing hatred and strife under pretext of defending victims of such hatred and strife. A daughter who believes she has forgiven her mother for wrongs done, nevertheless carries on a merciless warfare against her under pretext of love for her father. Another does the same, thinking that she is defending her sister against her parents, without realizing that she is carrying out her own vengeance in this strife.

In this way everyone projects his own rebellion into the noblest causes which he espouses. Each is leading his own crusade — so it is warfare on all fronts. Each allows himself to do wrong in the name of justice, and so justifies it. Every such act brings a reaction in kind from others, self-justified in like manner.

Thus nations feel they are victims of international injustice. Each thinks it will choke unless its demands are met: raw materials, access to the sea, colonies. Each denounces the other's wrongdoings and justifies its own in the name of higher justice. All of this brings on war, in which the nations suffer far more, and which sows injustice everywhere.

I want to avoid giving false impressions in these lines, or hurting those who suffer, by their thinking that I am insensitive to their suffering. Every day I hear the tale of the immeasurable suffering of men. I am under no illusions about this world, nor the injustice that is everywhere in it. I know that beyond all those attacked in the press there are those that are secret, uncountable. I know that fine people, religious and respectable, carry on in a way most cruel and unfair with their wife, their children, their friends, their maids, or their employees. I know that the victims often can say nothing because society is organized so as to protect the strong and find the weak to be in the wrong.

"*Summum jus, summa injuria*," repeats Dr. Dubois. I know that in a marital conflict, often the wife who has been wronged, and who is seen in the right as she denounces her husband's unfaithfulness, actually is responsible for this infidelity because she had contempt for him, and threw him into despair. I know that such is true of social and international conflicts, where the privileged can use the established law to cover their wrongdoing. "In this the company was legally right, but morally wrong," a journalist recently wrote concerning a strike.

I know that even in their delirium of demanding, there is in every complaint of the sick, an element of truth. It is useless to try to separate what is true from what is false in their suspicions. I know how people protect themselves against such accusations by showing them to be sick, even sometimes by shutting them up in order to silence their voice. I know that injustices originating in nature, in sickness, in bereavement, in heredity which saddles a life from birth, in accidents, in errors of treatment, pose questions to our conscience which we cannot silence and yet which we cannot satisfactorily answer.

The Christian is under no illusion about the evil that exists in the world. The Bible is not naïve when it condemns the shopkeepers' false balances, the Pharisees' hypocrisies, Judas' love of money, Pilate's pusillanimity, or the hatred of the crowd shouting "Crucify him!" Naïveté is rather to be found in our modern philosophy, which believes that it is enough to condemn injustice, to shout louder than the next person, in order to heal the world. The Christian knows that the depth of injustice's roots are to be found in man's heart, yes, in his own heart. He knows that in order to be freed from this, a divine intervention is necessary without which the best of intentions are useless, as are the noblest social reforms and finest legal codes. They can be twisted, too, only to serve evil.

Neither am I pretending that jealousy, lust, and envy date from today. Hippocrates, the father of medicine, wrote: "Man is full of illogic, empty of upright works, and supporting immense labors for no use whatever. He melts gold and silver, never ceasing to acquire such and always anxious for more . . . some to buy dogs, others to buy horses. They circumscribe a large region called theirs, and wish to be masters of vast domains when they have not even mastered themselves. They are in a hurry to marry wives soon to be divorced; they love, then they hate. . . . Possessing no riches, they covet them; possessing riches, they hide them, or dissipate them. . . . What they are looking for is that which is beyond their grasp: living on land, they covet the sea; living on the islands, they covet the mainland. Kings and leaders think the commoners are happy. The latter would aspire to kingship. The city ruler envies the tradesman, and the tradesman envies the leader."

What I maintain is that, though these passions have existed in all ages, in modern times they have been overactivated by our preaching of limitless demands. Here is a girl of a comfortable background, but who by change of fortune has to work as a maid. She is sick with resentment. Yet, I can see that she would be different if there weren't those good souls, who believing thus that they are showing love to her, constantly tell her, "How can you accept such humiliating work?" These are ways of defending the demands of the poor which actually push them down rather than uplift them, and which contain an implicit value judgment on their situation in life, worthy of a reactionary.

We have amassed men's bitterness by encouraging thus their demands. They've been taught a philosophy of chance which is similar to that strange doctrine of chance by which nineteenth-century science tried to explain the world's evolution. When we see no more than chance in what goes on, good or bad, we soon are engulfed by envy and bitterness. Those who draw up lists of grievances treat themselves to great popularity among the very ones whose misfortune they aggravate by accustoming them to nothing else besides their misfortune and by encouraging in them hopes that can never be fulfilled. We stir passions up to the point of civil or international war by persuading classes or nations that there are others who are happy, while they are not. And the war in turn stirs up the passions until all objectivity is lost. A noticeable exception to this was the clarification made by the Pope the day following the first bombing of Rome, in which careful objectivity was kept.

As a doctor I am called to show that the unfurling of passions during warfare is not any worse than that which abounds in people's private lives. After a certain psychoanalytic therapy, the children came and insulted their elderly mother because they were convinced that she was the cause of all their failings. Those children were doubtless "cured" of their inner hesitation, since every passion unifies the soul by seizing control of it. But they are not happy; they sow despair everywhere they go. Many have come to think, because of a false understanding of psychology, that they are victims only of others and never of themselves. In order to lead a normal life, they think they should have no complex, they should have had no emotional shock, no tribulation, no trauma. Nothing should ever constrain their free development; no external will should ever oppose theirs. They have been persuaded that every social demand provokes dangerous repressions, and that happiness consists in the absence of contradictions and pain — a philosophy which engenders suffering, because it is utopian. The Stoic pagans were closer to the truth by their demonstration of happiness in inner serenity, even in the midst of the worst catastrophes. Here is a patient who divorced her husband on her doctor's advice. Yet her life is much worse since, and her husband's too. They continue to see each other almost daily, for they still love each other. From fear of going against instinct, everything has been jeopardized by the whim of a moment. Every day I see people who, carried along by this all-pervading philosophy, come to realize the extent of their unhappiness and all the injustice of which they are victims. I plead with them to understand that my warnings do not mean that I consider their sufferings to be just or merited, nor that I minimize them, nor yet that I excuse or approve of those who cause their sufferings. I feel intimidated in their presence, since I am so privileged to be surrounded and encouraged by love. Yet, it is precisely because of my sympathy for them that I cannot refrain from saying what I see every day: that is, that those people are twice unhappy who live over, from morning to evening, the bitterness of their grievances.

I maintain that they are led astray by the modern outlook which has made a god out of equalitarian justice. "It isn't right!" That is the universal cry in whose name men draw up all their demands. They cannot understand us when we refuse to shout with them and they quickly suspect us of leaguing with injustice. They say to us, "You who are Christians, can you allow such a state of things?"

It begins in childhood when the school children return home their passions all heated by the discussions they've had together about some wrong a teacher has committed. The parents join them and become indignant that their child has not been fairly treated. If the child fails in school, the flood of

grievance develops quickly, and hinders the parents from seeing their own faults and those of their children. These latter,
already suspicious of unfairness in every teacher, bring such a
poor disposition to their schoolwork that they are naturally led
to further failures.

The parents become more and more irritated, considering
their son to be victimized by everyone. They plant such an
antisocial attitude in him that it ruins the remainder of his life.

Parents cultivate this false idea of equal justice also by cut-
ting up a cake carefully into equal parts for each child, large or
small, fat or thin, or by seeing that they allow nothing of one
that they deny to another. Thus the children are not prepared
for life, which is made up of inequalities. They unendingly compare themselves with their neighbor, to their own chagrin.

Later on in life in the office, the factory, the Army, the political system, everywhere, it will mean this carrying around
their unfair treatment which sows distrust, division, enmity,
and the thirst for revenge. Everywhere it will produce the cry,
" It isn't right." Everywhere justice will be invoked, as if it
were a god.

This does not mean that God is not just or that he does not
will fair treatment. But in abstracting justice apart from God,
in making a god of it, men have deformed the ideal of justice.
They have molded the modern idea of equalitarian justice so
much in contradiction with what nature teaches us, so much in
contradiction with the philosophers and with the divine Word.
For modern man, everything that befalls him, and that does not
befall everyone else, is unjust.

In inert nature, of course, everything tends toward a complete leveling, according to Carnot's second principle. But in
biology, the opposite is true: everything tends toward progressive differentiation of functions and individuals. Nature's justice
lies in that perfect harmony between complementary and unequal functions. Dr. A. Thooris speaks of the " equalitarian
poison " which brings on the masculinization of women and the
feminization of men.

For Plato, social justice was the same. It lies in each person's accomplishing his own function in the city, and in the respect of its laws. "Thus the city . . . is not a meeting of equal and like beings, but rather of unequal and dissimilar beings."

Naturally, I could quote many other philosophers: the tract "On the Delays of Divine Justice," by Plutarch, or Boethius' philosophical consolation, wherein we are taken from the apparent problems posed by the world's injustice to the contemplation of the unfathomable justice of God.

Justice in the Bible consists in the obedience of God. The just are those who seek his will. The justified are those who are delivered from sin by grace. By such a divine intervention in the heart of man, justice is able to come upon the earth. The Bible certainly gives us the vision of a golden age when "the wolf shall dwell with the lamb" and when "they shall not hurt or destroy" (Isa. 11:6, 9), but the Bible is not naïve to the point of pretending that this will come about through the grievances of the lambs. The Bible (Matt. 7:1), above all, tells us "Judge not." It sends each back upon himself and asks him to consider his own injustice instead of condemning that found in others. "None is righteous, no, not one." (Rom. 3:10.) Here we touch upon the central point of the conflict between Christianity and the modern spirit. The latter is concerned with the defense of its own rights, its unrewarded virtues, and the wrongs inflicted upon it. The former sees its own unworthiness, the unmerited grace it receives, and it holds out its hand to its brothers-in-misery. "Weak as we are, let us not have the audacity of judging the guilt of others," wrote Dr. Dubois. If the prophet is called by God to "denounce the wickedness of the wicked," Sabatier reminds us that Francis of Assisi well expressed the spirit of the gospel by adding, "Yes, the true servant corrects the wicked continually, but this he accomplishes above all by his conduct, by the truth shining in his words, by the light of his example, by all the splendor of his life."

"You're in a line-up at the wicket," one of my friends recently said. "You hold on to your place carefully, so as not to lose it: that is equalitarian justice. But if you give your place to an old woman, that is the justice of the gospel."

What I maintain, secondly, is that this whole tide of grievances which submerges our present world is useless. It does not achieve its goal. Am I exaggerating when I say that never was there so much injustice as there has been since so many people have gotten mixed up trying to bring about justice through their protests. Someone may answer, "Slavery has disappeared." I am not so confident that many of our fellow men are not just as ill treated as the slaves of yesteryear.

In any case, I can speak of what my own eyes have seen. I see lives literally saturated with grievances that, even when they gain their point in one matter, have so many more they want righted that they tire the best-willed people, deepen their own sense of isolation, and receive even more unfair treatment. I hear couples who come in turn to tell me of their grievances against each other. Let me emphasize again, grievances that are perfectly well founded on both sides. Each keeps track of all the sacrifices he has made for the other, in vain, and the bald-faced wrongs that the other has committed against him. In this atmosphere, happiness never comes back to them. They can patch things up for a while, through some momentaneous concession, but it doesn't last. Instead of coming together, they draw farther apart, and in their growing despair they commit ever more wrongs against each other.

Every grievance sets up a barrier between two persons, who can find a solution to their conflict only in fellowship. If the grievance is ill founded, it inflames indignation in the other, self-justification, and even spite. "Since my wife accuses me of infidelity, even though I am not guilty, why should I impose such fidelity upon myself? She doesn't trust me anyway." When the grievance is well founded, the result is no better, for no one likes to be in the wrong, no one wants another to put the finger on his sore spot. Outside of the miraculous climate of love, the normal reaction of any accused is to defend himself by attacking his accuser. "You criticize me today for my selfishness? Well, you've nothing to talk about! When I think that yesterday you weren't so interested in me because you had other friends. In your eyes I count only when you don't know what to do with your time!" Thus one grievance only begets another. They hold hands all across the world, for the husband who feels his wife's reproach passes it on in the mood of his remarks toward his employees, and so it goes.

The barrier set up by grievances does not exist solely between man and wife, but exists in the very heart of the one with grievances. A girl complained to me of her mother's authoritarianism. I suggested that she pray for her mother as the best way to help her mother to overcome her manner. The daughter replied that she could pray for anyone but her mother. She had too much resentment against her.

I see many wives and husbands desirous of "helping" their partner to overcome a weakness, disorder, or drinking, for example. But their zeal is not disinterested; it is simply so that they won't have to suffer the consequences any longer. The demanding spirit that is in their heart only alienates their mate and puts him beyond any good influence. Furthermore, the feeling of isolation that such demands create in him saps his moral strength, and enslaves him even more to his vice. In order to help someone to gain a victory, one has to be completely positive in his attitude. Before anything else, trust must be established. But the demanding attitude puts everyone on the defensive, and destroys trust.

Moreover, grievances sharpen one's critical attitudes. Here is a young woman who has begun to notice a degree of vulgarity in her parents' behavior. She saw in it a lack of respect for her — because they knew how to act in the presence of others. From that point on, she could no longer be intimate with her parents without inner feelings near the boiling point. Every common act or word made her most angry and hurt her as if it were personal. The parents, feeling their daughter to be so distant, allowed themselves to drift into an ever less careful attitude.

Here is the wife of a worker, completely rebellious at the material and social level at which her husband's work obliges her to live. In her grievance, she loathes housekeeping and neglects her home in order to read novels. Her husband, humiliated, seeks refuge in the coffeehouse, and their financial situation steadily grows more desperate.

Thus can we formulate this psychosocial law: complaining brings about that which is complained of. Here is a woman whose husband suspects her of not being completely frank. This soon creates in her a feeling of being "followed," and without even realizing it, she hides from her husband anything that might irritate him.

A girl was accused of theft, unjustly, as it was later proved by the confession of the guilty one. However, before the confession, the first girl was subjected to a series of questionings and suspicions which upset her and made her unable to clear herself. Despite her clear conscience, she felt the weight of moral isolation and of the suggestion "I am a thief." Later, when she found herself in great emotional tension following an unfair act against her, she turned almost automatically to the suggested weapon: this time she did steal.

"Good produces good," said Nicolas de Flue. Alas, evil also produces evil. Grievance produces conflict, and conflict sets into further grievance. I am struck by the great number of children who criticize their parents' faults and who then act in precisely the same manner. They behave toward their children, for instance, with the same severity from which they have suffered as children themselves. Their grievance determined their attitude, and gave the suggestion which later made them act in the same way. A young woman is bitter against her mother for having broken her engagement in order to keep her dependent. This grievance obsesses the daughter to such an extent that she can think of nothing else besides, and has thus fallen into an ever greater moral dependence upon her mother.

Here is a husband who did not find in his wife the love he had expected. Then he began to simulate adultery by being away from home mysteriously, hoping that jealousy would bring his wife back to him. It worked out the opposite way: the division between them only widened. Then, he was caught in his own game and became enamored of a woman. He is very unhappy, and feels more alone and more unsatisfied with himself then ever.

It is by such a chain of mutual grievances, retorts, and vindications that so many couples come to see divorce as the only possible escape from the grip of indescribable sufferings. In its turn, the high frequency of divorce undoubtedly contributes to aggravate the spirit of grievance in other homes. From the moment that one begins to consider the possibility of divorce, from the moment that the example of highly honored friends who have divorced encourages him to consider such an eventuality as legitimate, each offense of his mate wounds him more deeply, seems more intolerable, and excites in him the spirit of grievance, which leads him in turn to be unfair and hard.

Sometimes it is a silent grievance, a sort of strike; it takes hold of your throat and paralyzes you. Here is a couple who have spent months without exchanging a word at the table, and a crushing atmosphere goads on the grievance in both of their hearts. A husband gets to the point where he is glad when his wife falls sick, thinking that she is being punished for what she has made him to suffer. Then she feels rejected, and left to herself in her sickness; bitterness grows in her heart and she makes her husband suffer all the more.

Here is another couple the husband of which was full of suspicion with regard to his wife. He played the policeman. It was always a matter of questioning her about the use of her time. So the old story of Punch's making fun of the policeman was reenacted. The tracked wife took pleasure in thickening the plot, and gave her husband all kinds of false leads. He was the laughingstock of supposed witnesses, and in his humiliation, he redoubled his senseless worrying. He has become absolutely obsessed, which ever more poisons both their lives.

Grievances have their repercussion upon the sexual life of couples. The outflow of love, even the physical desire itself, is choked. With its disappearance, the other partner's sexual unsatisfaction comes to the fore. And this unsatisfaction in turn, especially when it possesses the wife and thus reverses the natural law of male initiative in love, only further paralyzes the husband. Nothing else, even in the subconscious, unlooses the torrent of endless grievances in the woman in every area of married life than the feeling that she is no longer sought after, that she can no longer conquer her husband by the attraction of her beauty. In other cases, it is the sexual problem which is at the bottom: a sensitive husband, inhibited by certain personal complexes in his sexual development, needs a very relaxed atmosphere in order to overcome them. Yet, his wife is all tensed up by her sexual demands, which further aggravates her husband's blockage.

All this takes unheard of proportions when the two partners are neurotic and bring along into their marriage a heavy burden of personal and hereditary problems and difficulties. At the smallest annoyances, even their love aggravates their grievances. There are endless lovers' quarrels, where each tries to make up afterward, where when the one says no the other says yes, and then in turn says no in order to get even with the first when he says yes. Each in turn is hurt and hurts the other; each suffers, loves, and yet hides his love; and each makes demands because he loves, and hurts the other because he loves. They consider each other as sick. The war of nerves continues until the moment an explosion in one of them permits his committal for care, and the other's obtaining of divorce. Or else the one commits suicide. Doctors see this too constantly and in all its tragedy to underestimate the terrible power of these series of mutual grievances. Even when one of the partners makes a gesture toward conciliating the other, he is misinterpreted, and his act produces the opposite result. If the other is not helped spiritually, his self-respect is only wounded, and again, by spite, he draws his spouse into a worse whirlwind. I helped a woman to come to the decision of breaking off with her lover. Her husband, instead of welcoming her back with open arms, only held her the more in reproach for her past. He refused to see me, and all seemed to be lost, until a friend of the husband intervened and led him to a spiritual experience.

Sometimes the source of our revolts are unconscious. One patient wrote: "I realize that if I used to dream of killing this friend, it was because I wanted to eradicate the wrong that I had done to her." Actually, we often bear grudges against others less for what they've ever done to us, than because of our indignation which has been stirred up and which eats away at us. Dalbiez gives the classical case of the psychoanalysts: the mother who gave up remarriage for her child's sake, and yet, despite all the affection she lavishes upon her child, unconsciously begrudges him for having hindered her from remaking her life. I have seen many such false sacrifices, albeit quite sincere, but which are not from the depths of the heart and which never extinguish the deep grievance therein. It is only covered up. Hence, many Cinderellas who appear sweet and self-sacrificing, and of whom we thoughtlessly take advantage, in reality, are in great inner tumult.

Discord rebounds from one to another. "When a conflict exists between two members of the same family," writes Dr. Liengme, "or of the same group, this first conflict engenders others. . . . The new conflicts engendered arouse in the principals the older, deeper, and hidden animosities which may long have passed from memory."

Dr. Dubois refers to insurance litigations, wherein "conscientious workers . . . know in advance that the firm responsible will try to reduce their claims, and to haggle over the indemnity," which simply makes them exaggerate their claims. In turn, this constant exaggeration on the part of the victims, whether it is conscious or not, forces the insurance company to a vigilance in mistrust. We all know to what unfair settlements this can lead. Likewise, we know what a state of obsession it can create in the victims, all of which hinders their recovery.

Our whole social life is based upon the deceiving fiction that justice will come out of a balancing of the opposite, exaggerated claims of those involved. The gulfs of separation are ever widened, everyone is embittered, and each denounces the other's exaggerations and uses this argument in order to stretch his own claims, lest he be foiled. Agreement is made ever more difficult, and injustice triumphs.

I could speak long, at this point, on jealousy. This elementary and primitive emotion plays an enormous role in all family and social relations. " Jealousy," wrote Cervantes, " sees with opera glasses, making little things big; dwarfs are changed into giants and suspicions into truths." How many married people there are, not just jealous of any friendship that their partners may make . . . so that they break them up one after another, but actually jealous of one another. If one of them has a certain pleasure or satisfaction, a business trip, for example, right away the other demands a trip too. So a system of bookkeeping is established, wherein neither ever finds the balance in his favor. They are always comparing themselves. The wife is jealous of her husband's intelligence; yet at the same time she is proud of it. The husband is jealous of his wife's social ease, and yet nonetheless proud of her for it. A husband is jealous of his wife's passion for the development of her magnificent voice; he wages such a guerilla warfare against her that she gives up singing. A wife is jealous of the interest her husband shows in his profession, or in politics, and she manages to ruin his career. Each of them bitterly demands the right of self-development, of cultivating his abilities, of enjoying life and of being useful. From jealousy, each of them clips the other's wings. Their home life is more and more impoverished.

Here is a delicate woman. She is jealous of her husband's health, and overworks because she cannot endure being idle while he is working.

How numerous are the fathers who are jealous of their children and of the affection the mother bestows upon them! How many wives of doctors, ministers, and lawyers are jealous of their husbands' clients! Their husbands just as jealously protect themselves behind the curtain of their profession. And the jealousies in work — those workers, nurses, employees, teachers, who cannot bear seeing a new and important responsibility entrusted to a colleague! We know of the jealousies among artists, and athletes, as well as those among politicians. Everyone can fill out this picture, everyone can repeat Weatherhead's phrase, " Jealousy — often we think it comes from a great love for the other person; more often it is from a great self-love." What I wish to point out here is this same vicious circle of grievance. Jealousy begets jealousy. It creates what it fears by forcing the envied partner to demand his right and his freedom, and thus to heighten the other's jealousy. It's a dead-end street, for like all the passions, jealousy cannot be quenched. Even if the husband does give up all his social relationships in order to appease his wife's jealousy, or if he strips them to a bare minimum, it does not change the situation any. Except through a spiritual experience in which this circle is broken, jealousy, grievance, and conflict will only further develop according to implacable psychological law.

Say, for example, that I am in military service. One evening there is a ball. Even though I don't care for dancing, I go along with my fellows in order not to appear to avoid their company. I dance, too. I tell it to my wife in my next letter. Her natural reaction, absent from me, is jealousy. " So while I'm alone at home, he's off having a good time!" Hence, I could quickly conclude that our mutual ideal of absolute faithfulness has become a trap for her, for it exaggerates her sensitivity. However, she spends time in God's presence; confidence and ease are reborn within her. This spiritual experience is possible precisely because in our ideal we have put God in the center of our marriage.

Jealous love crushes. Here is a woman who remarried after

having been widowed. Her first husband had more outstanding abilities than the second, and yet the second husband's abilities still make her feel inferior. Actually, it is not his talents that crush her, but rather his way of showing them off, stemming from jealousy. In another couple it is the wife who crushes her husband by her apparent brilliance. When he falls sick, she takes all his business in hand, and carries it on with ease. Apparently she has quick and brilliant success in all her undertakings. However, her successes are short-lived. For each time sickness interrupts as if there were an unconscious force in her, blocking the way to the intense effort inspired by jealousy.

This leads me to mention the basic grievance and claim — the one that seems adjacent and beneath all the others, whether these be international, social, or family-centered — the demand for affection.

There is in the human heart an inexhaustible need to be loved, and a continual fear of not being loved. Constantly, in all our human relations and in all our activities, we look for proofs of love from the other person. We look for them as remedies for our solitude. We seek others' reassurance. Those who doubt their own worth have a particularly insatiable desire for marks of affection because they just as continually doubt that others could love them.

Here is a patient who everywhere begs for affection because she was an orphan and bereft of maternal love. Here is another who destroyed her own marriage by exasperating her husband with her perpetual demand for affection. As a child she had been very sensitive, and irritated her parents. Their irritation made her doubt their love. Then she expected her husband to make up the deficit of affection. By her continual demanding, she exhausted his affection. Again she finds herself alone, her desire for affection twice as great as before.

In the accounts of their childhood that neurotic clients give me, the most constant theme is that of not having been loved by their parents. If we could question these parents, doubtless the father and mother would protest by enumerating all the sacrifices they made for their children. "We always were given money when what we wanted was love," a young woman told me. Another, a young man who had failed to turn up for an exam, ran to his father's office. He was made to wait, just like a client, and warned by his father that he was very pressed for time, even when he did get in to see him. Thus the son doubts his father's love, while the father is actually hiding his emotions under the cloak of business.

A young woman was raised by a governess, whom she detests simply because she took the mother's place. The daughter doubts her mother's love, while the mother herself suffers from the same doubt dating from her childhood.

A growing boy found his mother always too busy in the kitchen, where she sought to forget her own marital disappointment. He remembers the time, with intense nostalgia, when as a little boy on vacation he used to talk to his mother and she had time to listen to him. But he doesn't dare mention this to her.

A young woman admitted to me that as a teen-ager she simulated a long illness because it was her only way of getting her mother's care and affection, which she ardently craved.

Parents for their part seek just as many signs of affection from their children. They obstruct them in their vocations because of the children's desire to follow their own tastes rather than those of their parents, which is taken to be a sign of lack of affection. One girl who works all day in an office, and who is intellectually inclined, cannot sit down in a corner with a book in the evening without her mother's sigh, "So, you're leaving me all alone!" And the father who wants his children to respect his work actually is seeking their affection. One man offended his children by his behavior toward his wife, and they took her part in the divorce. He was desperately desirous of the smallest mark of affection from them. Behind all the legal disputes over the frequency of their visits to their father was this, his hidden despair. When they come, he smothers them in kindness, literally begging for a smile.

Between man and wife, the demands for attention and especially for time, consecrated to one another, are only demands for love. Here again we see the vicious circle; from being wearied into it, the husband will take time from his work for his wife, but in his heart he will begrudge her it. She will sense this, and demand ever more time as a mark of affection. A young man wanted to heal his fiancée from the wounds she had received in a previous friendship. Thus, he always came back to the subject, which turned into an occasion for quarrels. In his great hunger for love, he came to suspect that she couldn't free herself from her former boy friend, and so they quarreled all the more. A spinster who sees other women welcomed at the railway station by their husbands is deeply upset by seeing the couples embrace. How many lives dedicated to social uplift have as their secret motive a deep hunger to attract a gratitude sufficient to fill the void in their heart. Many people are always aching and complaining only in order to obtain a bit of pity which would take the place of affection, of which they feel deprived. In families, this demand for affection is mutual, and a mother and daughter can be seen living for each other, all the time in continual arguments. They spy on each other, waiting for a sign of love that might be seen in the other's sacrificing a personal preference for her.

The tragedy is that the very ones who most desire to be loved are the ones who create a vacuum around them. A fiancée who could think of nothing but the number of visits from her fiancé could not stand his being held up by his work. She lost her wits over it, dreaming up a plot. She wrote herself anonymous letters containing threats and then lodged a complaint against the unknown writer. She did all this in order to overcome her fiancé's excuses, and to force him to be more affectionate. When the police unraveled the mystery, the engagement was broken and the young woman would have fallen into despair had not a spiritual experience saved her from it.

One mother had an insatiable affective need because she had little faith in herself. Gradually, she wore out everyone around her who showed any affection. In her intolerable social solitude, she clung to her children. Her daughter was studying far away, at a boarding school. She asked her when she might phone her. The daughter, knowing that her mother's calls are long and that she cannot cut her mother off without hurting her, tells her mother that calls are not allowed. Later, when she unthinkingly told someone else to phone her, her mother was completely upset and felt less loved than ever.

It is very difficult to show love to these hungry hearts. Their very desire creates the barrier to any really affective relationship. So intensely do they want this heart-to-heart fellowship, and with so great fear of being deceived, that they lose the ease and relaxation in which warm feelings are spontaneously set free. They want so much affection, right from the first contact, that they cannot help but be deceived. And faced with deception, they withdraw into themselves.

I enjoy presenting a gift to my wife much more if it is a surprise to her. The same is true of all showings of affection: to demand is to lose. Thus the unquenchable heart creates its own vacuum about it. Such hearts discourage, successively, all those who, moved by compassion, try to surround them with affection but soon come to feel that there is no limit to the demand. If we spend an hour with them, they see only the hour which we cannot give them the next day, and reproach us bitterly for it. Their demanding makes them very critical of those close to them, and continually they suspect hostility and prejudice against themselves. The fact is that everyone ends up by turning away from them; their unconscious then provides them with a thousand-odd ills as a resource for commanding pity. Only by an inexhaustible love can they be healed. But where can we find such love? How many times I am forced to my knees to surrender to God the irritation that their complaints give me! For such irritation, inevitable as it is, will only deceive their confidence in me and give rise to further complaints.

The truth is that God alone can fill the affective need of men; God alone is always there, in his limitless love. Here is the case of a young woman, victim of wanderings hard to believe. Bit by bit she lost everything in life that might comfort her. An orphan tossed about from country to country, deceived by some and exploited by others, she ended up sick, in the mountains. There, she discovered a New Testament. She had never received any religious teaching previously. Suddenly she realized the immeasurable love of God for her; later, she consecrated herself to Christ's service. Her troubles are not over, nor is her manifest need to be understood and to be loved. The symptoms of this need are still misunderstood by some, and held against her. Nevertheless, in spite of everything, her faith has continually grown and given her courage. It has constantly quenched her affective needs. She has been able to live in her loneliness because she has found God with her there. In the fear of solitude found in our contemporary activitists, there is fear of emptiness — of an inner life, wherein God is absent. This is why men of faith are those who love to turn aside into solitude, and then return among their fellows in order to bring affection to them, instead of demanding it from them. "To love solitude and to hate isolation" is the slogan of the brotherhood of Christian intellectuals in Cluny.

II

The reader has already realized that our demanding not only poisons our interpersonal relations, but poisons our very souls. Its venom acts not just between persons, but in the personality itself. We need to demonstrate this more clearly.

First, it brings fatigue and tiredness. When we have joy in our hearts, in an atmosphere of confidence and co-operation, we can polish off a tremendous task without tiring. However, when we have grudges against our bosses or our fellow workmen, when we are soured by a job in which we see only monotony or stupidity, when we are eaten up by a thousand grievances, an immense tiredness comes over us. It, in turn, serves to multiply our grievances. We always feel extra tired just before holidays, because their prospect increases the weight of our work's yoke. When I am tired by neurotic patients, I discover that it is especially because of the hostilities that their troubles arouse in me. These resentments I try to repress, which absorbs a large part of my energies. Hence the fatigue.

Let us not exaggerate. There is a real, physiological tiredness involved in all work. God knows it well, for he has prescribed times for rest, which men do not always observe. Yet, there is a tremendous degree of useless fatigue in most of the overworked people who consult us. If I may put it thus, they are really tired, but psychologically, because of the inner friction of their hostilities.

Then, as has already been abundantly illustrated, hostility prevents us from taking proper care of ourselves. Here is a patient suffering from a heart disease. Her doctor advised her to move to the plains. But she is incapable of accepting a sickness that would thus break up her career and separate her from her family. Her doctor, concerned at her procrastination in moving away, sent her to me. He realized that doctor's orders are not enough. Unless this woman comes to accept her sickness emotionally, either she will remain in the mountain country and compromise her health physically, or else she will move down to the plains with great emotional resentment, only to compromise her health psychologically.

In the third place, demanding makes one more sensitive. He who in his heart protests against an injustice suffers all the more from it. By renewing its bitter taste in his mind, he continually brushes against his wound. Here is a young schoolmistress who has a hard time taking the high mountain climate, but all the more so because she is lodged in conditions which are a shame for the municipality. Yet I can see how her indignation at the slowness of the school trustees in answering her fair demands has made her more sensitive to the cold, and more susceptible to illness.

Another patient suffered originally from an organic trouble. However, her rebellion against the illness has made her more sensitive, in fact, more fainthearted. She fears lest a certain food be bad for her, and by power of suggestion she is unable to digest it. There are exaggerations in her fears, which are noticed both by those near to her and by her doctors, and these dispose them unfavorably toward her. She flouts their advice one after the other, or else she overcoddles herself. It is no longer possible to distinguish the physical from that which is psychic, in her case. If the doctor wants to show her the psychic causes, she sees only the physical, and feels that she is not understood.

Grievance and demanding lead inevitably to self-pity. To demand is to set forth one's sufferings in order to arouse others' pity. They are not always convinced by us, but we are quickly persuaded of our own unfortunate state. Here is a client who daily has to endure great physical and emotional pain. However, it is at least twice what it should be, because of her immense self-pity. Her doctor, realizing the limitations of technical medicine, sent her to me. In vain have I sought to get her to think of something else besides her ills and misfortunes. If I speak in this way, she suspects me of not understanding how she suffers, and her feelings of being misunderstood only aggravates her self-pity. For full treatment, I procured a Christian woman to be her friend who, by sheer devotion and love, has succeeded in breaking this self-centeredness and thus has brought some light into such a sorrowful life.

" To pity oneself," wrote Weatherhead, " is the most weakening of all emotions. We must be unpitifully honest with ourselves . . . a suffering exaggerated can be a form of self-love which does us no good whatsoever."

Such a warning coming from a psychoanalyst is very welcome, for alas, too often the other side of a beneficial analytical cure is self-pity, so easily set in motion by prolonged self-examination.

Thus every form of demanding one's rights, even those quite objectively based, brings about a sort of mental self-intoxication. Unless the demand is satisfied, it plows its furrow in the mind which it holds captive. We see such unfortunate people, worn out by a legal suit in which they have not been able to vindicate their rights. It would have been better to have lost it right away than to have lost years of their life in bitterness, and never to be able to regain their joy, not even after a victory which is never all that they had hoped it would be! There are some people so sensitive by nature that we must counsel them to keep away at all costs from anything having to do with court, so much psychic harm does the smallest judicial action inflict upon them. Such a person came to me one day, upset to the point of hallucinations. Her husband's lawyer had been practically threatening blackmail in order to get her consent to divorce. When I told her that she had simply to refuse any such demand, as well as any summons or correspondence, and that she could do so with no risk to herself, she blurted out, "That's exactly what my priest told me!" I saw her sometime later, quite calm and self-possessed.

If there are reactions of being upset to the point of mental derangement, obsession, and delirium, there are also reactions of coldness and withdrawal. That rigid and juridical turn of mind that Bergson attributes to the religion of law, and which he contrasts with the "dynamic religion" of Jesus and the prophets, is the result of demanding one's rights, which makes these "closed souls."

There is also the reaction of revenge. "At last I have a reason to live," wrote a sick girl in her diary. "It is to avenge myself!"

The mental self-intoxication by one's grievances goes so far as to reject proffered happiness. I see many people that, through their having suffered and having become embittered, have lost hope of happiness. They do not believe that they could ever possibly be happy. Grievance has somehow become such a mental habit that they cannot do without it. If they get their demands, they are completely disoriented. There is a leak in their soul hindering them from experiencing any happy turn that comes their way. Thus we see spinsters, for example, who are rebellious against their fate, but who when an opportunity for marriage comes their way, act as if they are driven by an unconscious drive toward sabotage. They act precisely in the way needed for them to lose their chance.

By sheer force of dwelling upon our causes for complaint, we lose sight of the brighter side of life. Often throughout my therapeutic practice I have thought of the story of the little girl who so wanted a brown-haired doll that, instead of being happy with the blond doll that was given to her later, she threw it to the ground and broke it.

In this way an elderly lady, because as a little child she never could accept the death of her father except as an injustice to her, has all her life had an attitude of having been wronged, which has destroyed every occasion for happiness. In the same manner, a man who never emotionally accepted his having been obstructed from following much-coveted studies has carried with him all through his career an inner rebelliousness that has hindered him from happy and fruitful work.

Bitterness related to lost loved ones is especially painful and difficult, for nothing can eradicate it except a spiritual miracle.

Here, let me express an idea which I hold very dearly. It is with hesitation that it is presented by me, because it touches upon a paradox, and therefore can easily be misunderstood: I have noticed more and more how dangerous it is for us to be right. The most fruitful hours in life are those of our humiliation, when we see our sins and wrongs, and when we are upset by them. Just as long as we zealously uphold a cause in which we know ourselves to be right, however, we remain inaccessible to any such inner feeling. How often I see husbands and wives, each in their turn! The one who is juridically in the wrong admits his guilt and is humiliated. Often I am witness to a truly spiritual renewal in this person, with whom I sense a real communion. Yet the other partner, because he (or she) is legally in the right, and because he thinks that forgiveness would be the same as approval of wrongdoing, remains quite impervious to any inner movement of a spiritual nature. I pity him far more than the other, since his bitterness cannot be relieved. If the two are seen together, one can only be struck by the contrast between their attitudes. The first neither complains nor reproaches, while the latter literally hounds his spouse, and laughs contemptuously at all promises of improvement.

One woman came to see me in order to tell of her marital disappointments. Her husband had started several businesses in which he lost money, one after the other. Meanwhile, she kept the household together by her hard work. She had oft forgiven him; they had talked things over; he had promised to amend his ways; she had each time tried to trust him again. She would have been willing to forgive him still if he were absolutely frank with her, as he had promised to be. However, she knew that he was still hiding something concerning his setbacks. She suspected them to be worse than what he admitted.

This time she had decided to refuse to pay her husband's debts. Instead, she wanted a divorce unless he was willing to accept terms dictated by her, which would have amounted to a tutelage.

The husband was quite likable. Confusedly, he tried to explain the adverse circumstances which had come upon him. I felt sure that if he had hidden this from his wife and had been caught in it, it was because he had been humiliated by her. She was a strong person, logical, one who broke his spirit because she was in the right and because she held his errors against him. How could I make her understand this? It was perfectly natural for her patience to have been lost. It was perfectly natural for her to want to set her husband right. How could I help her to see that it was this very attitude of hers which forced him to hide his business escapades from her.

However, she did open up to spiritual reality. She began to meditate and seek, before God, to discover her own failings. Months passed, with attempts at reconciliation, but none of them decisive. All were followed by fresh disputes.

It is easy to understand how moved I was to receive a letter from that wife, almost " out of the blue " it seemed to me: ". . . a miracle has taken place. I understand now that I was mean and self-righteous, that I made a change in my husband impossible. God made me see this, and has changed me. I asked to be forgiven . . . something I had never dreamed of doing, since he had always been in the wrong! And my husband was deeply moved, almost dumbfounded. He reacted completely differently from what I had feared; instead of taking advantage of my asking forgiveness, he asked me to forgive him too. . . ."

It is dangerous to be right, whether it is the young man criticizing the stiff formalism of his parents, the girl describing the intellectual poverty of her comrades at work, or myself, criticizing the materialistic attitude of a fellow doctor. Our criticisms are well founded, but the devil uses them to draw us into his camp. For it is in his camp that slander is heard, wherein there is no conviction of one's own sin.

Being in the right has always been a source of all kinds of intolerance. When we are right, we do not want to give in at all. We persuade ourselves that we are defenders of the truth. This is crystal clear throughout the church's history; the darkest pages of its history are those of its battles against heresy.

One day I had a dispute with a friend. I didn't want to give in because I was sure I was right. I am still sure I was right. But I was unhappy. I felt somehow that I hadn't lived up to my Christian ideal, which was to bring peace and not strife. In my inner turmoil, I took my wife for a drive and stopped the car on a country road. Inwardly I was very upset. After a long pause, my wife, who sensed what was going on inside me, said simply, "What are you waiting for?" I started the car and drove straight to my friend's home in order to ask his forgiveness for my obstinacy. After that I was overcome with joy.

I am scanning at the moment a dozen cases of men or women whom I have counseled in the past few years, persons that we might term " outsiders." From childhood up they have been the *enfants terribles* in their respective families. They see through all the little white lies that parents use to shield themselves from their children's indiscreet questioning. With amazing ability they sense the underlying meaning of the behavior of their parents, brothers, sisters, and their schoolteachers. They embarrass the teachers and make them uneasy. Intelligent, and generally ambitious, these children inspire in their elders both great hopes and great anxiety. In vain are they pointed to the example of their well-behaved brothers and sisters who play the game of social conformity and hence cause no worry. With them — the *enfants terribles* that is to say, there are incidents continually taking place. They accept no argument from authority; they argue every point tenaciously. The laughs are on their side, and their own parents, deep, deep down, often realize that their children are in the right. They favor life to regulation, imagination to conformity, and often their own heart to socially acceptable manners. They are admired by some and feared by others. The humble love them, the powerful fear their brilliance. They arouse jealousies and obtain favors, but they do not take root anywhere. Society shields itself from them and seeks to hold them at a distance by means of its formalism. Hence, their almost prophetic denunciations of society. They defend the hopeless, the outcasts and those crushed by society, the victims of injustice, and they remain lone knights in their armor, baffling in their perpetual tournaments. I have always felt deeply for them, for their paradoxical nonconformity, for their adventurous spirit always leading them into conflict with society and its torpor. They are impulsive, generous, unconventional. They are feared like the players who do not know the rules of the game, and who thus upset everything. They corner their superiors in the latters' mean gestures toward them, and send them scurrying. They don't stay anywhere for long. They leave by banging the door in contempt for those who have compromised themselves in a plot against them. Or else, they are fired for their impossible character. They are expensive for their families, whereas their brothers and sisters earn their own living within the channels of conformity. With all that, they experience moral awakenings like that of the prodigal son, bringing tears to their parents' eyes, and indignation to their brothers' and sisters' hearts, just like the reaction of the elder brother of the prodigal. I have known parents torn apart to the point of mental illness by this conflict between their children. They have been unable to give up their nonconformist son, a victim of so much social injustice, and equally unable to counter the rational argument of their other children.

In their impulsiveness, they err constantly. They marry by whim, and divorce the same way. They unashamedly live with a mistress, under pretext that it is much better and more sincere than to have one secretly like their brothers. They abandon their children to the grandparents, while they devote themselves to the care of other poor outcasts. Sometimes they know moments of brilliant triumph, but these are only momentary. They may be the family's glory and pride for a day, but more often they are their family's shame.

When we listen carefully to them, we have to admit that they are right in their great indictment. From them we learn a thousand repulsive details on what goes on behind the honorable surface of society. Nevertheless, they are neither happy nor productive in life. They go from conflict to conflict, from catastrophe to catastrophe, and even though they always may be right, they nevertheless sow division and strife wherever they go.

" One of our age's literary and psychological games," writes Thibon, " is to oppose ethics to life." However, these critics are more conventional in their rebellion than the social conventions they attack.

When they can be led to commune with themselves sincerely, they always confess the uneasiness deep down in their heart from which they suffer, the feeling of isolation which weighs down upon them, and their own pride in being nonconformist.

They are right when they denounce social formalism. Yet, in their reaction, they miss what there is of value in the moral traditions in which we are raised, and in which we find great security in our life. When one day I mentioned to a foreign client that I was a virgin when I married, he replied: "Apparently, that is possible in Switzerland. But, it is unknown in my country." Certainly I had no greater moral value than he, deep down in my moral attitudes; however, I am forever grateful to my social entourage, my forebears and my friends, who protected me against what are temptations and irresistible difficulties in other societies.

Here is a woman who came to see me after just such an adventurous and pillar-to-post life. She was again in trouble, this time with her manager where she had recently begun to work. She had followed the impulse of her heart rather than the rules of the office. After several interviews, she suddenly realized that her whole life had been twisted by her rebellion against her father. All her revolts against various authorities were but projections of her first revolt against paternal authority. He had been a religious father, well respected in his community. As a young child she had very clearly seen the hidden discrepancies in his life. Yet, just before her father's death, she was now able to go and ask his forgiveness. She settled down in her new position, gained her boss's confidence, and became much appreciated. Yet, she was still missing something. She realized that her father's formal religion had repelled her from Christianity and that inwardly she longed after a religious satisfaction. In the treasuries of Indian philosophy she found a way of drawing nearer to God. Far from alienating her from the faith, I noticed how much her deep Oriental spirituality brought her nearer, and I only waited for her to experience Christ.

Then one day she came to me, all upset. She had acted tactlessly toward her boss. All night long, she had not been able to sleep, because of it. She had turned to her father's photo on her table, and had seen with new eyes, so to speak. Now she felt herself, too, desperately despicable. No longer was she in the right, as she had been when she denounced society's sins. It was with a penitent heart that the next day she went to her pastor, to confess her sin. The latter spoke to her of confessing her wrong to her boss, just as she had expected. She was ready to do so, and so she did. Her employer received her warmly; all was forgiven and forgotten. What joy flooded her emotions! Now she felt that she had passed the greatest milestone of her life, that she had struck off at last in the right direction. She told me, " Now I understand why you were still waiting for me to develop spiritually."

Now, this woman's intuitive feelings and insight can be used to help heal the world instead of denouncing it, because she has herself experienced sin and grace, she has herself been to the cross.

When we are in conflict with others, it is always because we are in conflict with ourselves. " Those who are deeply virtuous," wrote Thibon, " are much less sensitive . . . to the lies and injustices of society."

One day I came to understand what the cross really means. It was after an automobile accident that I'd been in and that had cost the life of the man who had raised me. Some things in life can be put back in place, but others can never be put back. They would weigh down upon us eternally if it were not for Christ who died precisely to free us from them — and to make us new persons.

There is no other answer to the deep sufferings of people. One man whom I've seen on several occasions, unconsolable at the death of his elder daughter — now comes to tell me of his second daughter's death. Another patient, who because of an incurable disease has lost one by one all that he dearly held to in life, yet approaches death in full serenity, despite the many unsolved problems he leaves behind. There is no more impressive a testimony than such miraculous acceptance of life's tragedy. Take Francis of Assisi, for example, who according to Pius XI " had just enough body in order to keep his soul in him." Again, Alexander Vinet wrote: " The impossible is the best sedative. By chaining me down, God has accorded me all that good of which I would have deprived myself, had I been master of my own life." Augustine wrote, " Success is more dangerous to the soul, than is adversity to the body."

Above all, the cross is the only message to those in the torment of remorse, such as the father who cannot forgive himself for having failed to surround with affection his son, who now has been taken away by death. It is the only message possible for the husband who has just lost his wife, and who cannot forget how he caused her to suffer. Often I see people who, though they have borne their past wrongdoing to God in sincere repentance, still always think of it, and are in continual anguish. I have to make them face up to the cross, and ask them, " Does God forgive partially, or altogether? " This is the same question that my wife heard from the lips of her pastor, when a few months after my automobile accident, she went to see him to confide in him the great fear which tormented her, if the blood would be required of my hand on the Day of Judgment.

Here is a young woman, a leader in Catholic Action. No one fights for his faith in this world without being the object of a thousand wounds. It isn't just the adversaries who deceive you, but sometimes your friends, too. To think that even in the holiest of causes there is not missing compromise, unfairness, and underhandedness! The young woman has felt these and internalized them, so that her health is affected. She must bear all this weight upon her heart to the cross, to the feet of the One who was abandoned by all his friends in the hour of danger. Only thus can she be renewed for her ministry.

Christianity is not simply a matter of bearing one's cross; the cross must be borne joyfully. It is not simply accepting one's lot; it means loving one's lot, however difficult and painful it may be.

Here is a woman whose husband has left her. He is living in luxury with a mistress, while she is alone in poverty. Her own friends have given her up, telling her that she is stupid in refusing to give him the divorce, in persevering in her hope, patience, and solitude. However, this woman has a serenity which is most contrasting with the self-torture that I see in so many who demand justice.

When, day after day, we see how tenacious the spirit of demanding is, when all our efforts fail at disarming those souls who thus poison their lives and their surroundings in their fight, we no longer remain naïve. No longer do we expect peace to enter men's lives because we give them good advice. We know that an inner miracle is needed; for people to be reconciled, they must first be reconciled with God.

"When I see two brothers fighting, thus destroying their very human nature," again writes G. Thibon, "my sorrow is not just for them; it is equally for their common Father whom they first must have denied, before starting to quarrel."

If there are so many conflicts today, it is because of what Weidle has called the "great insurrection of man against God, which is the essence of modern history." This is the reason that man's revolt and grievances against all this world's injustice will never be displaced until they recognize the source of their revolt: their breach with God.

Then we come to see the paradox, strange and illogical, but true: we believers can see the accomplishing of God's plan even in those injustices which others may commit against us. This does not mean that God wants them to act in that way. But it does provide a greater and far more fruitful way of handling wrongs than the way of open battle.

Joseph, sold by jealous brothers to the Egyptians, told them years later when he once again saw them, "It was not you who sent me here, but God" (Gen. 45:8).

Here is a similar case of a young man, unjustly dismissed from the civil service while he was sick, thanks to an underhanded act. The medical adviser, whose report had been deliberately twisted, as well as myself, offered to intervene on his behalf. However, that would have meant an inquest and trial in which bitterness of soul might readily possess him. He answered us quite simply, in words of great depth: "If God breaks up my career in this way, it is because I refused to answer his call. Now, I'm willing to follow him."

III

Thus, Christianity opposes rebellion, and its entangling chain of grievances and demands, with acceptance, love, and forgiveness.

"Everyone has to suffer," wrote one of my patients." "How can one avoid bitterness? — by acceptance. How can one avoid repression? — by sacrifice. How can one avoid hating? — by forgiveness. How can one avoid anxiety for the morrow, and self-centeredness, and greed? — by self-surrender to the will of God. How can one avoid remorse? — by acceptance of its essential nature, and by repairing what wrongs one can. By Christian redemption."

In his letter to the "Generals of The Order," just before dying, Francis of Assisi wrote: "In this manner you will show your love for God, and for me your servant, and his: by there being not one sole brother in all the world who, having sinned . . . as much as it is possible to sin, and coming to you, can go away without having received your forgiveness. And, if he does not beg it of you, ask him if he does not want it. . . ."

This is an infinitely difficult message to take to those who suffer from inflicted injustices. One patient told me in her first visit that she hoped I would intervene on her behalf with one of my colleagues who had treated her unfairly. She was completely indignant when I spoke to her of forgiveness. She thought that I was actually afraid of my colleague. And I must confess how my heart is torn when a wife, who has been deceived, commits herself to the hard road of patience. Month after month I hear the story of her suffering, that her love has not brought her husband back to her, and that this test, showing no promise of soon ending, seems too much for her strength. But I know that she is really coming to see me in order to renew her courage and to be faithful to the end.

Here is another, also deceived and scoffed at by her husband. He silenced his conscience by deliberately mistreating her. She had often come to my office to renew her strength and perseverance. One day she said, "I am wondering if my leniency isn't just encouraging my husband in his bad conduct."

Christian forgiveness is not leniency. So much confusion reigns in this matter that I must underline what I have said; there is even a degree of contradiction between the two, forgiveness and leniency. Leniency pleads the attenuating circumstances, it tends to whiten the sin, to say that "it is not quite that bad." Leniency implies lying a bit to oneself, violating one's conscience in order to excuse others' misdoings. I am not saying that it is an evil. It is, in a sense, a very noble thing, but it does not bring any real relaxation, any real peace to the soul. Many who come to me, in order to appear lenient and charitable, speak to me at first very guardedly of the wrongs which they are suffering. They tell me: "I cannot give any details, for I don't want to say evil of my husband, or my boss, etc. . . ." I have noticed that with such an attitude, however noble it may be, they never get to the place where they can really forgive. In order to get to that point, they must first confess their natural resentment, just as it really is burning in their heart, and which they are trying to cover up. First they must get out into broad daylight the often enormous hostility, which they have repressed inwardly in order to appear bighearted. Only then, when the truth is confessed, and with God's help, can they forgive. Forgiveness looks straight at the wrong, sees it in all its wrongness, and then forgives precisely because it is evil — just as God loves us because and in spite of our sin, and not because of our good qualities. If there is nothing really wrong, if "it is not quite that bad," there really is no need for forgiveness. Leniency makes forgiveness impossible, unnecessary.

Here is a man who was suspicious of infidelity in his wife to the point of obsession and vexatiousness. The wife brought him to me for treatment. In vain she sought to reassure him, to take up each point in his accusations, and thus to clear herself. I proposed that they try another path. " There is no smoke without fire," I told the wife. " If you haven't actually deceived your husband, you doubtless have other faults to confess. The gospel says that anyone who looks at a woman with lust has already, in his heart, committed adultery. In the light of this, neither of you is really without sin. Instead of trying to prove your innocence, confess to your husband all that your own conscience accuses you of. Then, he will be able to forgive, because you will be no longer draped in self-righteousness." This couple did find the path to mutual trust.

Again, here is a husband who was trying to calm and reassure his wife. She had been expecting a baby. He had considered it dangerous for her, and had arranged for its termination. He had even kept his wife from coming to see me for fear that I might dissuade her from it. Now she was greatly upset. He offered her all kinds of explanations; he sought to convince her with a thousand arguments that the abortion was legitimate. But his wife's troubled condition grew steadily worse.

" There is a real and deep guilt in your wife," I told him when he came to my office one evening, " and without doubt, in yourself as well. You are trying to reassure her in order to reassure yourself. You know very well that you have disobeyed God. Start over by confessing it along with your wife; then each of you will be able to receive God's forgiveness which is promised to everyone who will admit his own wrongdoing." To cover up or deny is to obstruct forgiveness. Two days later, I received a wonderful letter. This couple had truly experienced the reality of forgiveness.

Often I have met another kind of confusion. A woman, for example, noble and bighearted, naturally inclined to forgive and excuse many of her husband's failings, nevertheless believes that she must be unyielding when it is a question of marital infidelity. This rigidity of attitude may not be from a sense of being hurt, but rather from fear that her forgiveness might be an approval of evil itself. Yet the word of the gospel is clear: "Love bears all things, believes all things, hopes all things, endures all things" (I Cor. 13:7). The popular distinction made between those lesser sins which can be put up with and the more serious ones which cannot be pardoned is completely at variance with the gospel. Only when there is a real wrong can there be real forgiveness.

Christian forgiveness likewise is quite different from a certain kind of Stoic pardon with which many confuse it nowadays. Here is a husband, who in an Olympian tone of serenity says to me: "Oh! I don't hold it against my wife; it doesn't bother me; I have learned to maintain a spirit of good will through all the mishaps of life." But I sense that he has not really forgiven his wife. Many of his attitudes and words only betray an inner turmoil from which he is seeking to protect himself.

Thus true forgiveness begins by recognizing the evil and by confessing our natural reaction of anger which it always arouses in us. Then, when both the evil action and the feeling of anger are borne before God, forgiveness and the recovery of our inner peace become again possible.

Again, here is another lonely soul, full of grudges against her family and against many others. Deep down, I think, she would gladly forgive. However, she waits in vain, and it is her own life that is being poisoned by this waiting and bitterness.

Here is another one, just as embittered. Actually, she had been cruelly mistreated. Her career had been ruined by unfounded suspicions. I knew this, and I knew also that there was no other answer for her than to forgive. Yet I gave up hope of leading her to that forgiveness. Then, one Sunday she went to church and a quite simple remark made during the sermon struck home to her. She felt that God had spoken personally to her. She was so joyous in her new-found freedom that her sister asked if she had fallen in love!

With regard to asking forgiveness, many people mislead themselves. Here, for example, is the case of a woman who wrote to her husband, "If I have wronged you in any way, I ask your forgiveness. . . ." She was quite surprised that her husband didn't reply in spontaneous and bighearted affection. She thought that she had asked to be forgiven without realizing that the " if " took away from her letter all that it contained of heartfelt contrition. She knew very well that she had wronged her husband, but she sought forgiveness without clearly admitting wherein she had wronged him. To apologize is always a hard thing, and we are ever tempted to tone it down. Especially is this so when the other appears to have wronged us more than we have him, and yet shows no indication of regretting it. You will understand, then, how I felt when I saw a woman, deceived and abandoned in sickness and poverty by her husband, write to him sending a small sum of money which she had kept secretly from him, and asking his forgiveness. This woman was truly happy.

We can achieve Stoic serenity or bighearted leniency by working at it. Not so with Christian forgiveness. Forgiveness is never anything but a gift received from God. Here is a woman who also was the victim of flagrant injustice. It tore away her social career into which she had poured her whole heart. She was discredited by a real intrigue against her, and even some fine friends turned their back upon her. She came not only to doubt all that she had ever believed, but her own worth as well. Nevertheless, this great trial began in her quite an inner evolution; she began to seek for God, to pray, to obey inner inspirations. There were a few moments of happiness, but the struggle was far from over. She could not overcome her resentments. She asked me, " What must I do to be able to forgive? " I had nothing to say to her, for there is no human technique for manufacturing forgiveness. However, I suggested that she ask God for this, and I assured her that God would answer her. Many months later, she came into my office just radiant with joy, and burst out, " It has happened! " One morning, when she was least suspecting it, an indescribable calmness had come over her. She now saw those who had made her suffer in an entirely new light. They were unfortunate ones, who like herself, probably had great doubts of their own worth. In any case, they too were fighting that inner tragic battle common to all men. Perhaps she could help them now. At least, she wanted to with all her heart. There was the authentic accent of Christian love in her words. She added, "You know, I was quite skeptical at times when, month after month, you calmly told me that there was nothing I could do but wait for God to give me this forgiveness for those who have wronged me."

It is always those who have the deepest hurt to forgive who forgive the most completely. Hatred and love are two emotions very, very close to one another. If we symbolize hatred with a negative quantity, $-n$, forgiveness is not just the cancellation of the wrong which would create an emotional neutrality, o; rather, it is a change from minus to plus, in quantity. Forgiveness is the replacement of hatred by love, $+n$. He who cannot hate intensely cannot love deeply. Thus the same intuitive insight which tracked down the wrong in all its wrongness, can also come to see the tragic state of the guilty conscience. "To understand everything is to forgive everything." A patient of mine came to see that the repulsion she has felt for her mother came from her discovering her mother's same "lack of balance" in herself.

It is thus that a woman whose husband is psychopathic has been able to carry on, to take everything from him effortlessly, by seeing in him the tragic psychological struggle in which he is caught. Leniency comes from an effort. Forgiveness is a miracle. Forgiveness even brings about the eventual forgetting of the wrong.

Yet, it is better to forgive by an effort of the will than not to forgive at all.

I like very much the idea of starting over again from zero, as with a cash register. Thus forgiveness brings about the cancellation of past debts and attitudes. Because a father failed to forgive his older son for the worry the son had caused, the father begins the training of his younger son "in the red," so to speak. He surrounds him with a mistrust that plunges the boy into sickness. Because another young man cannot forgive his friend for the great disappointment the friend has caused, he can no longer get close to anyone without the injustice of suspecting unfairness in him. Forgiveness is what Dr. Liengme calls "immediate liquidation," which he makes into a rule for living: "Learn to forgive . . . do not allow the roots of bitterness, fear, jealousy, impatience . . . to develop. . . ."

Thus Weatherhead speaks of "this amazing therapeutic agent, the doctrine of forgiveness. . . ." To be able to forgive gives such a relief to the soul that it is all the remedy that many neurotics need.

The forgiveness must be real, not just a façade. It seems to me that when an injustice is done to us, we have three ways in which we can react. We can return tit for tat; i.e., we can make the injustice bounce back again. We can abstain from returning the same in kind, but without forgiving, either; this means internalizing one's anger, rebounding the injustice within us, repressing it. Finally, there is the way of true forgiveness; this alone can break the chain of evil.

Here is a patient suffering from chronic eczema. Following a certain mental relaxation, the eczema all but disappeared. Then suddenly the dermatosis made an acute comeback. The patient was able to discern its cause: one of her boarders tricked her in a deal with his ration cards. In order to appear bighearted, she never said a word to him about it. Her indignation, instead of being discharged, was kept within her, ever accumulating. Therefore, if we do not get rid of our anger by returning wrongs suffered, we must find the spiritual way of ridding ourselves of it, that is, forgiveness.

To a sick woman who had suffered from countless conflicts, I said one day: "Life is like a tennis game. It never finishes if you always return the ball. If you can forgive, then the balls can come your way without your having to send them back."

An elderly lady, a widow, came to see me. She was a very small person, but with sparkling, soft eyes. She had lost her only son through an accident; one of his chums caused his death through carelessness. One day she was thinking that this boy must be troubled with guilt and remorse. She visited him, to tell him that he was forgiven.

A young man, a cripple, was in prayer. The idea occurred to him to visit the doctor, who by an error of diagnosis had contributed toward his now incurable state.

In our world of misery wherein there will always be suffering, forgiveness is the only way to reconcile men. It frees us from our passions' enslavement, and allows us to regain objectivity.

"True friendship among all nations," writes Dr. Missenard, "means that each nation must really accept its neighbors as having to be different from it."

True peace, without heaven-sent forgiveness, is an impossibility. Pius XII has stated it well, "The sword can very well impose conditions for peace, but it cannot create peace."

Can nations forgive? Doubtless, as with every other spiritual gift, forgiveness in its essence cannot be other than individual. This, as I see it, is where all the conscientious objectors are in error; they do not distinguish between individual and social ethics. If a man, in order to follow Christ, accepts the risk of Christian nonresistance, he accepts it for himself, and has to bear its consequences, even if it means a cross. However, when he wants to impose this risk upon a nation which is not as a whole converted, he is fleeing his responsibility in that community where God has placed him.

National demands are aroused by the goading of a few leaders who draw the crowds after them. In the same way, a few men who have personally experienced Christ can communicate a spirit of forgiveness to the nation.

In our national history, we know how a Nicolas de Flue was able to receive the necessary authority and vision, in his daily communion with God, in order to restore peace to our confederation. (Translator's note: Nicolas de Flue was the Swiss counterpart to our Abraham Lincoln.) Méautis says that de Flue wrote to the government of Bern, "Peace is always found in God, for God is peace, and this peace cannot be shaken. Discord, however, will always bring us into further troubles."

Later on, General Dufour, by the spirit of charity in which he executed the heavy responsibility of putting down by arms the revolt of a few cantons, contributed to the consolidation of our national community in the most fruitful way possible.

In order to bring peace to others, we must have it in ourselves. I see many people who never forgive themselves. In their holy ambition to be perfect, they are cruelly disillusioned by their own failings. By failing to forgive themselves, they become bitter with themselves. This negative inner attitude throws them ever into new failings.

Let us, like Francis of Assisi, ask of God this spirit of love and forgiveness:

> Lord, make of me an instrument of thy peace!
> Where there is hatred, let me sow love.
> Where there is offense, let me sow forgiveness,
> Where there is discord, let me sow unity,
> Where there is doubt, let me sow faith,
> Where there is error, let me sow truth,
> Where there is despair, let me sow hope,
> Where there is darkness, let me sow thy light,
> Where there is sadness, let me sow joy,
> O Master, let me not seek to be consoled as much as
> to console, to be understood as much as to understand,
> to be loved as much as to love.
> For it is in giving that we receive,
> It is in forgetting ourselves that we find ourselves,
> It is in forgiving that we are forgiven,
> And it is in dying that we are raised up into
> eternal life. Amen.

VI

The Spirit of Fellowship

I

Does all this mean that we are to turn our backs on the social injustice and evil that pervade our world? Does it mean that in our families, schools, economics, and politics our bighearted forgiveness must allow selfishness, greed, and violence to triumph unopposed? Of course not! Christianity simply proposes a different way to bring in justice. It is a much more effective way than that of resentment and retaliation.

Abundant illustration has been given of the vicious circles of "just" demands, of jealousy, and of loneliness. They are so striking that the scientist cannot fail to notice in them a natural law: fear creates that which is feared; complaining aggravates the condition that causes it; demands poison our conflicts and our conflicts harden our demands; and isolation leads to further isolation. Yet, there is another side to the same natural law: trust begets trust; forgiveness disarms injustice; love creates fellowship and fellowship resolves conflicts; and an open and sincere attitude integrates the person into the fellowship, wins the hearts of others, and lifts them out of their emotional isolation.

Not always! We have to admit it. It would be underestimating the power of evil to pretend otherwise. It would amount to presenting Christianity with no cross. There is in this world so much evil, and in mankind such an interdependence, that no one can escape the effects of evil. Some of these effects are ours by nature; some are ours because of others; some are ours because of our own actions. They are multiplied for those who live in revolt against their lot, and they are present in the lives of those who seek the way of self-surrender. But whereas the rebellious contribute to our world's sickness, the self-surrendered take part in its healing. The former's troubles are never resolved; the latter's lead them to personal victories.

As I write these lines, I am putting in my annual military service. (Translator's note: Annual military service is obligatory in Switzerland for all male citizens of a certain age group.) In the mess, after our coffee, we are having a " bull session." Quite naturally, we talk about our world — its scandals and its sufferings. We talk much about our generation's deep disappointment at the failure of all the efforts made to establish peace and a just social order. We remember what all our leaders have promised us, whatever their political stripes: peace and fair dealings among the nations, justice between social classes, and a fair deal for the family.

One of my officers won the approval of all present when he declared: " The error is in trying to remake the world without remaking man himself. Changing our laws won't achieve much if men aren't changed within."

" But can man be changed within? " someone will ask.

The Christian faith says yes, and gives many indisputable demonstrations both from history and from present-day experience. It is conscious that evil will always be with us in this world and that a really new world will come only with the return of Christ. However, it does not await him by sitting with folded arms. It knows that the changing of one man always produces social repercussions. It knows that when a young child in his family, an ordinary worker in his factory, or an average citizen in his country commits himself unreservedly to the way of loyalty, purity, self-surrender, and love of Christ, he transforms the atmosphere around him. He awakens the feeling of fellowship and influences even those who criticize him in order to ease their bad conscience. How much more is this true when an intellectual, a plant manager, a journalist, or a politician undergoes this inner revolution which Christ brings! This is why their responsibility is much greater.

Yet this moral influence of the transformed individual upon his milieu is not the only social effect of Christian conversion. A sincere Christian cannot be indifferent to evil social institutions that obstruct justice and fellowship. He must work for reform. Only, now he no longer does this in the spirit of demanding his rights; he does it in largehearted service.

We like to contrast the reform of man with the reform of social institutions. Both camps do this. One camp says: "Look here, there was never any greater revolutionary than Christ; yet he never attacked the institutions of his time, such as slavery and Roman imperialism. He was satisfied to call men individually to his salvation. We would waste our time if we entered the endless political disputes, for all social systems are bad."

Others tell us that it is but idle talk to speak of changing man. If a few souls here and there experience a profound conversion, so much the better; but they are exceptions to the rule. In the meantime, the whole world is prey to the cruel injustices of its institutions. Thus, so they add, the proponents of social reform are really more Christian than the proponents of individual salvation, because the former throw themselves into the fight for reform while the latter quite comfortably theorize on the regeneration of individual souls.

Such an argument appears to me as quite fallacious. Like all our intellectual dilemmas, its choices are artificial. There is no answer to the problem so long as each side continues to point out its adversary's errors and its own good reasoning. Again, we need to synthesize rather than to analyze and divide. We need to recognize the truth in both positions.

Christianity has become much too indifferent toward society's institutions. We have bound up society's wounds and cared for its victims, but without going back to the causes of such suffering. If our faith is to bring an answer to the troubled world of today, and Christianity alone has the answer, then we must lead the way toward social ideals and institutions that conform to the pattern of the community that Christ gave us. At the same time, such a reform will be useless unless it is rooted in the personal spiritual experience of many individuals. To change the world, we must be changed men.

In one of his devotional works, Dr. E. Stanley Jones has strongly underlined this dual aspect of the Christian faith. There is an inseparable relationship between individual change and social reform.

How, then, can we work for the reform of social life without falling into the trap of "just demands," which we have already exposed? The answer lies in the turnabout, the inner change of direction that is part of true Christian conversion. The individual and his clan are people who want to receive what is their due; the person and the team are people who want to give. To demand is to ask from others on behalf of oneself; Christian service is to offer to others from that which is ours. To demand is to combat the evil in one's fellow man; the Christian warfare is the combat against evil in oneself.

The biologist knows that life is a struggle. The smallest cell can survive only if it protects itself against its environment, assimilates from the environment what it needs, and rids itself, in that environment, of what it no longer needs. Therefore, the biologist cannot conceive of absolute peace here below as meaning anything other than death. In order to live there must be struggle. If this struggle is external, it pits us against our fellows. It isolates us, creating conflicts that ever grow more serious. There is thus only one solution: to turn the conflict inward, to make it a struggle within oneself.

For several years I very zealously and sincerely waged a fight for the reform of certain institutions. I proposed revisions for the federal constitution as well as for that of my own church. All of this, in spite of my good intentions, brought me nothing but disputes, divisions, and misunderstandings, and put me in the disadvantageous position of a critic. Some people feared me, some congratulated me, many opposed me. No one came to me to open their heart to me, to ask me for help, to seek in me strength and inspiration for living a better life.

Then one day a man, by speaking to me of his own failings, helped me to realize that all the while that I'd been discussing the reform of our world, I was tolerating many compromises in my own life. It was then that I passed through the gateway that alone makes a life fruitful: the gateway of conviction of one's own sin, and confession.

Many people confuse the conviction of sin with such feelings as inferiority, scrupulousness, lack of self-confidence, and so on. Yet, whoever observes people closely can see that these feelings and the conviction of sin are not only different from each other, but are in certain regards mutually exclusive. A diffuse and vague guilt feeling kills the personality, whereas the conviction of sin gives life to it. The former depends on men, on public opinion, while the latter depends on God. The former is related to our social formalism and its marks of esteem, which have nothing to do with the true value of a person. Hence a guilt feeling leads to self-contempt. Conviction of sin, however, is linked to the respect of oneself as a creature of God. When I feel my sin and am shaken because of it, it is not at all because of feeling inferior to others. It is because one of God's master-pieces has become stained by sin.

Thus it is that Christian experience first of all restores the human person and then spreads out from person to person until it transforms society. Christ, after having preached to thousands, concentrated his attention upon a few disciples. It was to this handful of men that he confided the enormous task of taking his message to the ends of the earth. God's method throughout all of history has been one of personal calls. He calls a Moses or a Francis of Assisi, a Paul or a Karl Barth, to a life of rugged obedience, from which self-discipline all their spiritual, social, and political ministry flows forth.

Our civilization is obsessed with numbers, statistics. We love loud-speakers. We believe we can save time by enrolling everybody at one swoop. We are essentially bureaucrats.

Christianity forms leaders; it forms their convictions and conscience. A business man who through obedience to his conscience breaks with that dishonest practice which is general in his firm, and who says, " I will no longer do that, no matter what situation arises," is a leader. His action is more effective in bringing justice than our countless petitions covered with signatures. A worker, such as one whom I know, who dares to invite his boss home with him in order to offer him help in changing the moral atmosphere of the shop, is a leader.

Christianity, as well, offers such leaders the resources of grace, of daily fellowship with Christ, for the inner renewal needed in order to face the obstacles and traps that lie in their path. Here is a visiting nurse who has given herself to social work from a sense of calling. She realizes one day that the widespread immorality that she daily witnesses is haunting her imagination and poisoning her soul. She needs to empty her heart in meditation in order to begin her task afresh, renewed. Often I feel that I've been influenced by the patients whom I wanted to influence, that I've been taken captive by their spirit of criticism or their love of intellectual discussion. I need to be renewed every day in the presence of Christ. How many men there are who have thrown themselves into politics from a sense of calling. They were adamant against the too-common compromises of their environment, but now they have been drawn bit by bit into doing as all the others. No one can clean a dirty object without dirtying his hands. Therefore, it is necessary for us to be able to wash them, in order not to dirty what we next must touch. The soul is purified in the face-to-face encounter with God.

Likewise, Christianity assures us inner serenity — protection of our person against the surrounding anxiety. " When we bear peace within us," wrote Maine de Biran, " we can meditate and do things in a thought-out way, even in the midst of our world, whose agitation we do not share. However, when we are inwardly perturbed, everything distracts us, and the deepest solitude fails to calm us."

Again, the man who has passed through the Christian experience is freed from the parliamentary spirit. Because he has dared to face up to himself, he no longer fears men, nor does he fear to discover their true selves behind the social mask they must wear. Like Socrates, he tests not their ideas but the men themselves. He brings into being thus, with his friends and with his foes, an atmosphere of fellowship in which agreement, instead of endless disputes, is possible.

I do not wish to reflect upon the intellectual life here. Personally, I am thrilled by intellectual concepts. Yet, I know also how greatly I was long enslaved to the love of discussion and debate. Likewise, with those who come to me for consultation, I often take note of the subtle trap into which their brilliant intelligence has led them. It has allowed them to juggle with the basic problems of life without their ever having committed themselves. Self-commitment is always the decision of our heart; only when our intellectual life is under the sway of our heart can it be fruitful. "Intelligence is never fulfilling its role," writes Father Sertillanges, "unless it accomplishes a religious function, that is, it must worship what is ultimately true, that which is both in and beyond the limited and immediate truth." "Dialectic," said Pierre Damien, "must not arrogantly claim for itself the right of the master. . . . Rather it must be the servant of its mistress, faith."

This is the price that thought must pay in order to be reintegrated into life. Denis de Rougemont has shown, in *Penser avec les mains*, how great a divorce between intellectual life and real life has taken place in our modern world. Those intellectuals are countless today who suffer from this divorce and do not know how to heal it. They do not know how to make the transition from abstract debates to thought-out and practical action.

Nevertheless, the greatest of philosophers, Plato, always united, even in his own mind, intellectual speculation with the reality of social life. His greatest works are at once both philosophical and political. He believed completely in the social mission of the philosopher.

The separation of thought from life has its roots deep within us, for we have become accustomed to distinguish between our belief and our behavior. So effective is the distinction made that we no longer see how contradictory the two have become. To regain consciousness of this contradiction is to experience the conviction of sin, which in turn re-establishes the unity of knowledge and action. This is the condition that must be met if our political and social debates are to become a mutual, loyal, and creative search, a search that unites us rather than a dispute that ever divides and pits us against one another. It is generally believed that political opponents are divided by questions of principle. Actually, the most bitter opponents are brothers at war, and that which divides them is emotional hostility, jealousy, grudge, and pride.

To be set free from the spirit of dispute is also to be freed from the mania of giving advice. Advice is the only form of social activity of which many are capable of conceiving. Those whom life has wounded have met givers of advice on every hand. Often the advice is good, but if they follow it, they remain children. If they do not follow the advice given, they are isolated. Often they are surprised that I do not give them any advice. They would prefer at times to be led rather than to assume personal responsibility for themselves. Thus I patiently apply myself to giving back self-confidence to the client who has completely lost it. It is very important that he dare to affirm his own personal conviction. Yet his parents may jibe him, "What good is it for you to see the doctor if he doesn't give you any advice?"

Advice may put people back together again, but it cannot change them. "Advice which can touch only upon the manner of action," said Ariston of old, "can never transform the soul and set it free from its false opinions." Advice touches the surface of personality, not the center. It calls for an effort of the will, whereas the true cure of souls aims at the renewal of the inner affections. "With regard to therapy," writes Dr. J. Loebel, "we must get down to the very sources of life in order to get hold of the whole person, to understand the man as he is, to grasp the form and the living essence of his being."

I interview husbands who give their wives all too much advice, wives who do the same to their husbands, and parents to their children — all with the noble aim of helping them to overcome their failings. To give advice is to place oneself above one's fellow, thereby obstructing the spiritual fellowship in which alone he can be helped. The best way to help one's wife or husband to make headway in life is to go ahead oneself. When the children become particularly difficult, the parents have only to ask themselves what is wrong within, and to correct that. I see many people who would like to solve a marital problem before having solved their most elementary personal problems. "In order to give yourself, you must first be self-possessed," Vinet used to say. In order to build a strong home, we need to strengthen ourselves first. A certain woman had deep marital problems. She was all the more disappointed because several times she and her husband had opened up to each other and had thought that their differences were resolved. At the same time she recognized that these were efforts of good will, without any profound change having taken place in her personality. She couldn't understand herself. Now she saw that first she would have to seek an answer for her deep religious anxiety by deepening her faith. Faith alone can break our inflexibility.

In dealing with couples in conflict, it always seems to me that the real problems are not between them, but in each of the partners themselves. If each is set free by an inner experience, no marital problem is left, even if their differences of taste and ideas, which seemed to divide them, remain.

It is in this way that the social action and behavior of a person really depends upon his inner experience. The first step in every fruitful social action takes places in the soul. It is precisely in the person's making himself available for the benefit of others, that is, in the surrender of his personal considerations. A young woman who was very sensitive and shy, and who secluded herself with her personal diary, unburdened herself to others after a spiritual experience. Thus she reintegrated herself into society and found her vocation. A teacher embittered and discouraged in her work made the great discovery of God. She threw herself back into her life which thus became a thrilling experience for her, and her pupils were captivated by her teaching. Another, a nurse, discovered that if she had been disappointed in her career, it was because it had not made up for the bitterness of her relationship with her parents. She had tried to run way from it by taking up nursing. After her reconciliation with her parents, she was able to enjoy her work again.

II

In the Christian concept of society, the individual's relationship to the larger community is seen in terms of vocation. Each person accomplishes his life purpose to the degree in which he fulfills the function to which God has called him, and to the degree in which he does so according to the will of God. Not only that, but society's purpose is fulfilled at the same time. Social justice, then, is precisely this attaining of our life purpose.

It is striking to note that, in an age of troubled minds just like our own, one philosopher, Théodore Jouffroy, was most deeply preoccupied with this problem of life purpose. He could not escape the idea that " no being in nature has been created in vain, that is to say, every being has its purpose, its calling, its mission." However, led astray by the proud philosophy of his time, which claimed that philosophy had replaced our faltering Christian faith, Jouffroy tells of his emotional crisis, in which one night in December, 1813, he realized that he had lost his faith. Thus, he held that no one can know what his life purpose is.

The fact is that apart from faith, man's life has no meaning, and there is no standard for society. Today we stand at the end of the age of great unbelief that was then just beginning. We are able to see how great the confusion has been into which both the individual and the culture has been plunged. In order to restore both the person and the community, simultaneously, we need to return to the Christian concept of vocation. Each person, in the light of revelation and in spiritual meditation, may make out step by step what it is that God expects of him. Naturally, he often makes mistakes. He goes forward in trembling, and has to feel his way through the midst of darkness. Yet, despite all this he feels led and has a sense of contributing toward the bringing in of divine justice, according to the degree of his obedience. Also, he gains self-confidence. The talents he has received are for him an indication of what God's plan for him is. In this plan, they will bear fruit for society's benefit. How often I feel heartsick in the presence of sterile lives. They are like " frozen assets " that serve no purpose and that can be reawakened only if faith gives them a social purpose. This is just as true of peoples as of individuals. Thibon writes of his country, saying that " she will recover her purpose only by rediscovering her God."

This concept of vocation unifies personal and social purposes. One day, a teacher who had come to see me remarked, " I have come to see, by reading your writings, that my difficulties arise from the conflict between my personal life and my profession. My profession is most satisfying to me, but not my personal life."

On the other hand, many others become very skeptical about their vocation. They see it only as a livelihood, and become reconciled to taking what little pleasure they can from it from day to day. The vast majority of people with whom I speak are discontented and disappointed with their profession. They no longer have any interest in their work or any conviction about it. Let us pause to consider how serious this matter is for our present-day society. As soon as a man takes God seriously, he takes himself less seriously and takes up his vocation and his responsibilities conscientiously once again. He quits being an amateur doctor, an amateur husband, an amateur father, an amateur public servant. When we are disappointed with our work, we are generally disappointed in ourselves because of the way in which we are doing our work.

"Yet," many answer me, "I have asked God to show me my vocation, and my request has not been answered."

To have a mission in life, one has but to bring a missionary spirit into the task at hand.

"Every human task is noble when a human soul throws itself completely into that task," wrote Marshal Pétain.

I regularly interview those who dream of accomplishing some grand and noble task, and in their waiting neglect the humble duties at hand. They forever remain uncertain as to their vocation in life.

In the same way I have seen many others who have remained uncertain because they saw themselves, theoretically, in a dilemma before two possible professions, and demanded of God that he give them a precise command in order to settle the question. They refused to begin answering the very questions they asked of God, questions that God had well enabled them to answer.

Most people who ask us if they shouldn't change professions are simply in revolt against their lot and want to escape.

On the other hand, I have seen men who by faith accepted their situation and their work as a calling of God, and who, because of their faith, put their whole heart into it. Their experiences were most fruitful, and through them these men were led gradually to new callings in which they recognized God's plan for them.

The really important thing in life is not the avoidance of mistakes, but the obedience of faith. By obedience, the man is led step by step to correct his errors, whereas nothing will ever happen to him if he doesn't get going.

"A doctor who discovers in himself the soul of an explorer," writes Ch. Beaudoin, "will doubtless do better to apply for a post in some overseas territory than to head off for the jungle himself. Even better for him, he may consider the challenge of research as his field of exploration."

Personally, I believe that in every case of professional orientation there are two questions: that of one's felt calling, and that of the framework within which he may fulfill it. In most professions each person is able to find adequate room for his personal bent. One doctor, for example, may seek technical perfection, whereas another finds a field of action for his practical intuition. A third may enter the field of scientific research, and a fourth man may develop a philosophy of man. Each man is equally serving his fellows, provided he has the same faith in his vocation and has consecrated himself to it.

One young man who wanted to be a doctor failed in his Latin exams. It was then that he realized what he had been looking for in the medical field: first, to escape the technical career his father wanted for him, and second, to work with people rather than with things. He came to see that this second desire could well be fulfilled in a managerial career.

Psychotechnical examinations can help a man greatly toward discovering the talents God has given to him. Like everything that is technical, however, these examinations must be kept subordinate to inner conviction. Strong conviction of one's calling has always seemed to me to be the greatest single element in a successful career. No psychotechnician would ever have advised Demosthenes to become an orator!

Many lives remain unfulfilled because of a lack of courage in affirming one's inner conviction in spite of all obstacles. One doctor, a bit tongue-in-cheek, told a nervous young woman that she would never have the health necessary to enter the nursing profession, the career to which she felt called. Yet, her nervousness was the result of just precisely her lack of self-affirmation. Her health grew worse and her inner discontent grew deeper from having allowed herself to have thus been blocked. Her uncertain and aimless life became far more tiring than any nursing career could have been.

By our fellowship, we can help others to distinguish what their vocation is, but we cannot have the conviction for them. Nor can we, from the outside, know whether their idea is an escape or a calling. Even when someone comes to realize that in his vocation there was an element of escape, nevertheless he can by faith see in it God's will for him. It is in meditation that convictions are hammered out and that courage is received to follow them.

Meditation broadens the horizon of one's thinking. One watchmaker discovered in meditation freedom from the failing, common to his profession, of seeing everything as small. Perhaps our watch industry has spread throughout our people this professional failing, so that we all have a limited outlook. Perhaps our mountains have contributed to this also. We Swiss have no access to the sea, no open door to the outside world. Keyserling has shown how the specific Swiss characteristics are rooted in our instinctive self-defense against Europe. One Swiss woman who had long been in India felt that she would suffocate back in the atmosphere of her homeland. Almost all those who have been in Africa have expressed similar feelings to me. One young foreign woman who had traveled extensively and who had studied in our land felt the silent hostility of our truncated society, which was incapable of understanding her. In my own city, when the League of Nations was here, there was a very clear line drawn between the Genevan city and the international city. The line was dented here and there, but not much more. We failed miserably in our mission. If Switzerland is ever to fulfill its mission in the world community, we shall first have to be healed of our defensive attitude. This does not mean that we need to dismantle our national defense. No one can serve the larger community if he fears to be truly himself. But the defensive attitude is nothing other than fear, fear of being swallowed up by others, fear of losing one's identity. Meditation leads to the discovery of one's true self and to self-confidence. It gives one a clear vision of what he has that he can share with others, and heals his fear so that his own worth is affirmed at the same time that he is led into a positive attitude toward the rest of the community.

We continually mistake instruction for thinking. As soon as a man begins to commune with himself, even though he may have had little formal education, he discovers that he can make his brain work just as much as the intellectual. He realizes that he can muster his imagination and his creative thinking to the service of his community. He is no longer limited to criticisms. We must admit it: mental laziness is one of the most widespread defects of our people.

A young woman, very discontented with what seemed to her humdrum work, came to see me. Now, her father was an intellectual, quite a brilliant personality. I realized that the idea had never entered her mind to talk with her father about her vocation, to learn from his experience and thus to broaden her own outlook. She surely needed such a larger vision. Most people, after they're twenty-five, keep in a closed circle of habit and thought. They become hostile to everything new and challenging from the outside, particularly because they might be forced to revise their ideas and to hammer out a valid, personal opinion. They learn their trade and, even in the liberal professions, then settle down into their little professional rut. When they are asked the fundamental questions of life's meaning, of history and world events, they answer that they realize all these things to be important, but that they don't have any definite position on them. After all, what can you expect? We don't have time to think; we are taken up with practical life! What is this "practical life"? It is a routine way of doing things that remains essentially unscrutinized.

Meditation, then, broadens the horizon of our thought and imagination and prepares us thus for our social role. It turns life back into an adventure. We never see anything in this world except what we are inwardly prepared to see.

Again, the practice of meditation gives a spiritual meaning to everything. God is not interested only in theology. He is interested in cooking, in medicine, in art, in sewing, and so on. Taken this way, no work is drudgery. And then, if as is the case in certain production trades, specialization has emptied the monotonous activity of any interest, the worker's interest can be reborn when he becomes conscious of what C. F. Ducommun, in *Pierres d'angle de la reconstruction nationale,* calls "the vocation of the group." It is the idea of belonging to a group that has a real and fascinating purpose in society and that one can serve by his thought as well as by his brawn.

I have interviewed many people who contrast in their mind a vocation that is by definition spiritual — such as that of a pastor, a deaconess, or a missionary — with their own lay vocation. They often feel that their own secret sins have disqualified them from such noble callings. As if sin is any less a serious matter in "secular life" ! We need again to recognize that God is calling all of us to serve him in the station of life where he has put us. This is what gives meaning to all of life and to every calling. This is what preserves us from the "rut of the disillusioned."

Many young women contrast, in the same way, career and marriage. Usually their professional achievement is pretty ordinary. They don't marry either. They become disillusioned about their profession, and disappointed as well at not having married. While waiting for marriage, they live a sort of provisory life that goes on indefinitely. They never put their heart completely into their work. When their chances for marriage are fairly well in the past, the feeling that they've wasted their life plunges them into depression. On the other hand, the ones who are not always thinking of marriage, but who pour out their mental energies into the work at hand, find themselves taken away one day by marriage! Those who do not give themselves wholly to their work when unmarried, because they think that they can do that only for their eventual home, generally make mediocre wives and mothers when they are married. The others bring to their marriage the same spirit of devotion that they've already applied as single women, to their vocation.

The same can be said of the mental opposition made between home and career by so many working wives. Meditation helps them too, by enabling them to give hour by hour their very best to what they've at hand to do. For God never asks of us more than one thing at a time. The inner conflict of our several responsibilities exists because we set our various tasks in opposition to one another. Moment-by-moment obedience to God is the unifier of all our duties.

The renewal of the spirit of fellowship through shared meditation, husband with wife, brothers with sisters, young men with young women, helps also to broaden the horizon of the woman's understanding. By nature she tends to see the concrete details, whereas the man is drawn toward the over-all theory. Both need a continual sharing of thought for their mutual enrichment.

Many husbands withdraw into themselves, claiming that they cannot talk with their wives about the really interesting matters. If they mention some social or professional concern, they feel that she doesn't listen and that she thinks only about her immediate problems. All this time the wife complains that her husband never says a word at home, whereas with his friends he is a fascinating conversationalist. By nature, the wife wants her husband to talk — for in his talk she seeks proof of his love — but she is far more interested in the fact that he is talking than in the content of what he says. On the other hand, the husband is interested in ideas, and if his wife is not enthusiastic about them, he finds that there is little point in exposing his thought. Thus I incline toward believing that this misunderstanding is more often the husband's fault, because he has not been able, by the power of his love, to broaden the horizon of his wife's thought and to awaken within her many new interests.

There is generally a feeling of inferiority in the wife, a preconceived idea that she can't understand anything in her husband's professional and political interests. She can be freed from this erroneous idea through meditation. As a matter of strict fact, a husband is not looking for any technical competence in his wife. This he already has in his colleagues and associates. Often he can even become quite angry if his wife tries to talk with him about his business as if she were his equal. But he does want her to show an interest in his life, very much so, and the center of his life for him is his professional activity. Men generally need their wives much more than the latter suspect, since because of masculine pride husbands try not to show their need. The social role exercised by the wife through her creative influence upon her husband is simply enormous. For this she needs no technical competence. All she needs is to love him and to love everything that interests him, that is, to be in emotional and intellectual fellowship with him. In this way she also integrates herself into the larger community. She is more often than not more intuitive than he, and in their shared moments of meditation she may have fruitful inspirations for her husband's career. But this attitudinal revolution is just as necessary in the husband. He, too, needs to realize that in spite of all his powers of reason, his technically ignorant wife can intuitively come up with suggestions that are well worth his trouble to take seriously in his professional life.

One of my friends, a Frenchman, spent a few weeks in our home several years ago. He told my wife about one of his friends, who was the manager of a large factory. This friend's wife used to spend a few minutes daily in meditation upon her husband's professional task. She had often had quite helpful inspirations for his work. From that day on, my own wife gained a new interest in my medical career. My own work has benefited just as much as our home life.

Here is a young woman whose husband had been active in politics. When she began to commune inwardly with herself, suddenly she realized how much interest and effort he had put into it. She had been blind to this interest of her husband's because she had seen his public career simply as a rival that was taking her husband away — so much so that she had succeeded in bringing his career to an end.

Many men in the more demanding careers, such as business or medicine, live with a perpetual conflict between their work and their home. This tension weighs down upon their whole life and reduces their effectiveness at work. They are caught between the demands of their wife and those of their business. They don't know how to allot their time to each. Feeling misunderstood, they withdraw into themselves. In order to maintain the peace, they account for their time occasionally to one side or to the other, but this never really satisfies either. Often their wife comes to detest their profession and their activities, and the groups to which they belong, and holds against them the time and money they put into their politics or their avocation. Here is the case of one wife who told me that for years now she had prayed in vain that God would give her a love for her husband. When we had talked a little we soon saw that she despised every one of her husband's outside interests. They were to her nothing but nasty rivals for her husband's attention!

Here is another woman who is at war continually with all her neighbors. She keeps her shutters closed all day for fear of their curiosity. She dreads the return of summer when she will once more have to attend to her garden — despite the fact that she has planted high shrubs all along the enclosing fence. I have discovered that the deep-down root of her obsessive condition lies in the disgust she feels for her husband. She is ashamed of his trade; she is ashamed of him. Her shame is projected into her hypersensitivity toward her neighbors.

The conflict between the demands of social vocation and home life is resolved through the mutual sharing of husband and wife in meditation. The wife can thereby associate herself in spirit with her husband's responsibilities, and the man can become aware of the domestic anxieties with which his wife has to contend. In this way both are enriched, and in return their wider horizons of concern enrich their shared meditation. It prevents the couple from developing a joint self-centeredness — or an affected mystical sympathy. For the woman, her husband's work becomes a part of her as much as it does a part of him. She is able to see the time that he consecrates to it as no longer being taken away from her. Conversely, the cares of housekeeping and children become a part of her husband, just as much as of herself, and he no longer sees the time she gives to home life as competing with professional and social demands he must meet. Above all, couples that achieve such sharing have experienced fellowship in the down-to-earth realities, which in turn helps prepare them to contribute the spirit of co-operation to the larger community. They can express themselves to each other. They are able to confess their shortcomings and to come out of this experience strengthened and set free to face their respective responsibilities. Sometimes I marvel at it: so many people coming to me for spiritual guidance, and myself needing the same from my wife!

A couple can help each other to be more faithful to their ideal and more honest with themselves. This is one of the deepest satisfactions possible in married life. They are enabled to complete one another and to make up for each other's weaknesses, as in the old fable of the blind man and the paralytic. Thus a frail woman who quickly tires out can achieve a great deal simply by inspiring and supporting her husband. Thus alongside the philosopher Alexandre Vinet, who was limited by his physical sufferings and family tragedies, as well as by his natural slowness at work and a marked lack of self-confidence that made him unfit for action as well as hesitant, there was his wife, who gave confidence to him, in his natural hesitancy, and ministered to his inner needs.

Finally, couples can also in this way harmonize their tastes and their ideas, rather than pulling each in his own direction. Instead of opposing each other on every decision that must be made, through this communion they can seek to know the will of God, which generally is entirely the idea of neither the one nor the other.

It is well known that an appendectomy is less dangerous if performed when the patient feels well rather than during an acute attack. The trouble is that patients often won't come back once the attack has subsided. Since they no longer " hurt " badly enough, they are no longer concerned enough to prevent a recurrence of the attack by undergoing the operation. In the same fashion, there are couples who never explain themselves to each other except when an incident provokes a crisis between them — when anger and wounded pride make them both say too much. In such situations, their discussion alienates them farther rather than bringing them together. Such discussion is both dangerous and insufficient. These couples come to us at such times. Each partner, rather than seeking a real reconciliation, is looking for a referee who will judge in his or her favor and condemn the other's unfairness. In these circumstances our own efforts are rather beset with dangers, and generally prove insufficient to the need. Once the crisis is over, when the couple could well explain themselves to each other without being blinded by passion, and could reconstruct their close relationship so as to be prepared for harder days ahead, they do nothing. They remain mute and show no concern. We see them no more until the next crisis comes. Employers and workers similarly never talk over the questions that have to do with their mutual concerns until there is open conflict that sets their passions aflame.

Fellowship, the true sense of community, is formed day by day, especially in the better days. It requires time, perseverance, and hard work, just as does the formation of a good football team. The players of a team are enabled thus to work together more than ever, and to face the rugged trials of their sport, instead of disintegrating in mutual recrimination and criticism.

It is all very simple, in theory. In practice it is very difficult.

Many couples have the ideal of fellowship at first, but after a few years they come to believe that it is impossible to achieve. I have even known couples who had at one time achieved such a total communion, only to lose it later on. They have both nostalgic and embittered memories, very serious obstacles for any new attempt on their part. They fear the suffering that any new failure will bring. It appears to me that very often the trouble has been that the one who feels more advanced spiritually has used the practice of joint meditation to dominate the other. He has crushed the other by his authority and reason, has been giving the lesson rather than listening, and has been humbling the other by pointing out his or her faults rather than confessing his own. He has discussed in order to prove his own point, rather than for the purpose of seeing his spouse's point of view.

Such blundering is quite common, even among those who love each other deeply and who have both faith and good will. Thus apart from the grace of God there can be no durable spiritual communion between a man and his wife. Yet, if the condition for such communion is grace, grace is likewise its result, bringing with it right relationships — more surely than any demands for justice ever could.

Here is a husband and wife each of whom is undermined by serious psychological complexes, but neither of them has ever doubted that their marriage is God's will for them. This certainty has been the great lever allowing them to face up to and overcome their difficulties in mutual adaptation.

There is a striking kinship between love and religious mysticism, so much so that even illicit love has at times been seen to rekindle the flame of faith within a soul. This upsets many people, who become very skeptical as to the authenticity of such faith. Personally, I think we have to admit quite unapologetically this kinship to be a fact and recognize that it can serve the devil's purposes just as it can serve God's — as is the case with everything else in life. In the intention of God, this kinship is to assure the fullness of marital love, which can blossom to its fullness only if at the same time it feeds upon and is fed by spiritual communion. Berdiaeff has spoken of this " spiritual phenomenon, which is quite distinct from the psychological phenomenon of sexual satisfaction, or the social phenomenon of the family."

Countless are those couples who secretly long for such spiritual sharing, but who do not find the way. They even fear to express their longing. Going together to church gives only a partial satisfaction.

The tragedy is that we find here once again the paradox mentioned earlier. Often the very intensity of the couple's desire for spiritual fellowship is what keeps them from being open and natural with each other when it comes to religion. A certain uneasiness hovers over every attempt they make toward a common spiritual life. The uneasiness hinders the fellowship. Here is a Protestant couple who for long have wanted to pray together. In her nervousness, the wife begins with a Catholic-type prayer, which completely upsets her husband. All that she really intended it to be was a way to hide her deep feelings.

Most serious of all, the desire for spiritual communion, when unsatisfied, often feeds a spirit of reciprocal demands and drives the couple apart. Here is a woman who has had a tragic past. One day when deeply in despair, she met a man of faith who completely upset her and brought her to faith. She married him, thinking that she could begin a new life with him, for she had recognized that her failings of the past were due to her alienation from God. Now she is completely disappointed in her husband. As a fiancé, he spoke so well of spiritual things, but now, faced with the real problems of marital life, he has withdrawn into himself. She is disappointed that he is so shy now and that he no longer plays the religious role she expected of him.

Others I have seen who, inwardly convicted by a spiritual call, hesitate to compromise themselves and thus remain in the sterile position of a divided soul. They fear having to explain themselves to their wife (or husband). They fear not being understood. They fear above all that their own spiritual obedience will alienate their mate. Generally it doesn't work out this way, for timidity and a bad conscience, together with cowardice, make for a far deeper moral repulsion.

Or else the spiritual life becomes a ceremony apart from living, without real contact with practical matters. These matters remain, therefore, untouched.

Other couples have, both of them, so much religious zeal that they fall into spiritual jealousy of each other. They compare themselves and judge each other, thus erecting barriers between them.

I do not wish to give any formula for a spiritual life, for everyone has to work it out in his own way, under the guidance of his church. Spontaneity is the condition of spiritual life. Therefore, as Plotinus, the philosopher of unity, said, it " must not be a purely formal and empty unity."

Whatever their situation, couples sincerely desirous of having a spiritual foundation for their marriage will be able to attain it, even through many errors. They can always turn to God and ask for it. To do so together is already the first step.

" The other day my husband asked me to pray with him," wrote a young woman to me. " I have felt ever since that moment that we have made a big step toward each other."

There is only one kind of marriage that is really creative: total marriage. In it there is achieved bodily communion, emotional communion, spiritual communion, and, if I may so express it, a communion between these three kinds of communion. Everything is shared together: interests, disappointments, victories and shames, money, worries, work, housekeeping, children, and social and spiritual vocation. There is no secret between man and wife.

Many marriages are heading toward the rocks because the couple were married with certain mental reservations. They wanted to maintain a certain part of their life apart from their mate. Or else, as often happens in educated circles, they have not obeyed the gospel commandment that orders the husband to leave his family in order to cleave to his wife. One or the other in the couple has kept father, mother, or perhaps sister or brother, as his or her nearest relative spiritually. Or else, again, the wedding has been only a legal way of acquiring a mistress. It has not been the total giving of self one to the other, for life. One woman had this to write in her well-kept diary: " I am continually perplexed at the flagrant inconsistency that allows a man to play the game of love with his wife, to make her his housekeeper in order to assure his own comfort, and yet to exclude her from being his friend, one with who he shares his inner life."

III

I have used the experience of marriage to illustrate the possibilities of the restoration of fellowship. Marriage is at the core of all social change. How can a man bring the spirit of fellowship into his office or into politics if he has not progressed that far within the framework of his own family? " Do not be led into error by any system of thought detached from life," wrote Jeremias Gotthelf. " It is not the state, neither is it the school or any other public institution that forms the person; it is the home. Those who govern do not make the country, nor do the teachers form its life. It is the fathers and mothers. What is really the determining factor is the home life, not public life. That is what supplies nourishment to the roots of society, and the fruitfulness of the tree of society depends upon the quality of its roots."

" The great task of education," wrote one pedagogue, " is to teach the child how to live in a community." We cannot do it unless as man and wife we have first achieved a truly shared life.

Like the ancient philosophers, especially the Pythagoreans, like the primitive church, like the first team of Friars Minor, we too can experience a true brotherhood which, far from weakening us, strengthens us by recognizing our true worth in our social calling. This is possible in our families first, and then among friends held together by a common faith.

What is particularly striking in our modern society is that our leaders are so overloaded with responsibilities and detailed work that they no longer have time for thought and meditation. On the other hand, where there is teamwork, confidence, the very capacity that we have lost, is placed in everyone. Each is put to work; each learns to carry his share of the load. When Nicolas de Flue intervened in the Diet of Stans, he did not consider it necessary to leave his meditative vocation or to appear in person in order to make his views prevail. He entrusted this to Im Grund, his confidant, whom he sent in his stead.

True team life, in which complete trust in each man's convictions is the order, in which the common task is accomplished with both order and freedom, is nothing less than a revelation to the modern man. In such a team experience each member assumes his own responsibilities according to his inner inspiration, so that each fulfills his own calling within the over-all fellowship. This is just the opposite of the present-day tendency of the masses to expect everything from a few overworked men at the top. To experience team life means that when there is a divergence of views, the problem is resolved by a common seeking for God's solution, undertaken in love and mutual loyalty. When I experienced this with friends from many lands and social backgrounds, and of many age groups and religious beliefs, I saw in the concept the social philosophy that our modern world so badly needs in order to get out of its individualism and its impersonalism, its formalism and its division.

As I am writing these lines I am reading an article, by Georges Duhamel, that recalls my memories of Place de la Concorde, in prewar Paris. Countless automobiles would cut across that square in every direction, yet without accident. Each driver, in one glance, would judge the position, speed, and size of all the other cars, and would decide between which cars he would cut across. Duhamel emphasizes the impression of discipline that the whole picture gives. Yet, no policemen or traffic lights were there to enforce such discipline. Duhamel's protests against the all-powerful technical organization of our modern world are well known. He contrasts the discipline that is created by each individual's judgment to that which is imposed from without by rules, or by traffic lights. He calls it " traffic controlled by mutual consent," for as we have noticed, there is true co-operation between all the drivers. One brakes a bit, and the other speeds up slightly, so that there will be no hold-up in traffic. Duhamel calls it "individualism," and he hopes that the "future lawmakers of his unhappy country" will build on this concept. But we need to agree on our terms. To me, the picture just drawn represents true teamwork. It is the kind I have experienced myself, quite different either from self-centered individualism or from socialistic leveling. In such team experience, instead of the individual's being set over against the group, team members find their fulfillment and purpose together, in a harmonious and mutual relationship.

I personally believe that our own Switzerland, where everything is small — commune, canton, even the confederation itself, as well as our industries and business organizations — is the country that has been prepared to demonstrate such an experiment to the world. It is at the grass roots, beginning with small groups, that a spirit of fellowship can be reborn. The biologist knows that a healthy organism is like a harmonious federation of complementary organs, that these organs are a harmonious federation of cells, that the cells are a harmonious federation of molecules, and these molecules — of atoms, and the atoms — of electrons. Plato's city, Rousseau's state, and Fourier's phalanx were intended, in the thought of their authors, to remain small communities.

Our country does not always recognize its immense privilege in possessing a federal structure, nor the mission in our world that this has placed upon us.

It is in work that today it is so important to apply our federative spirit, in order to restore the sense of fellowship in this domain and to save it from the chaos of competition. Before our eyes a new social philosophy is being set forth, equally free from the errors and excesses of liberalism as it is of communism. I will limit myself to pointing out the bold and clear thinking of C. F. Ducommun, who said that we must teach once again to all who work in a given enterprise that they are interdependent and complementary even though their functions may be quite different. Let me recall the beautifully simple picture drawn by Hippocrates, that penetrating observer of humanity. "When men saw wood, one man pulls toward himself while the other pushes; yet they actually do the same thing. Opposite movements are necessary if the saw is to cut through the wood. If the two men tried to use their strength without harmonizing their activities, chaos would result."

However, the experiments in "industrial harmony" of these latter years have shown the futility of drawing on paper a method of co-operation for managers and workers. First a spiritual revolution that will lead them back into personal relationship with one another must take place in their hearts. Joint committees have been established for the purpose of studying together all the inner problems of a given profession or trade; yet they have hardly ever met, and such meetings are less and less frequent. On the other hand, in those cases where bosses, workers, technicians, and employees have rediscovered the spirit of fellowship through a spiritual conversion, positive experiments have been made that have put an end to competition, rivalry, hostility, and mutual misunderstanding. If this is really what we want, if each no longer fears that the other is trying to trick him, it is not hard for us to find the tools we need for a more just society. The question is whether we want to rediscover God's will as it relates to our work.

Such a new spirit would not be long in renewing our political life. "What is the foundation for the life of a city?" asked Nicolas de Flue. His answer: "Love."

We have become accustomed to thinking that a Christian culture must of necessity be liberal, that is, that it must be competitive. Rather, it should be co-operative.

Recently I was talking with a medical student from France. He was intrigued by my spiritual experiences, and talked with great enthusiasm. When I asked him upon what solid foundation France could rebuild its life, he replied right off, " There is no other foundation except the gospel."

As for the international scene, Dr. O. Forel, in the work alluded to earlier, declares that " the present confusion favors a revision of our knowledge of the psychological laws that govern our affections and desires." Fear, as he points out, after so many centuries is still the great fact of human existence. Fear is the mainspring of all political organization and of all alliances. At the same time, fear contains the seeds of every conflict, whether it be personal, social, or international.

Now fear is an emotion, and only other emotions can deal with it: trust, love, faith. The hope that peace could be organized by the means of reason, analysis, technique, the progress of law, and the wise solutions of experts was part and parcel of all the illusions and prejudices of the age of unbelief from which we are now emerging. Our age thought that by excluding the supernatural a solid culture could be built that would be free from uncertainty, and therefore a source of limitless progress. The emptiness of this myth is plain for all to see.

We are proud that our country's representative to the League of Nations was opposed to welcoming men who openly professed hatred of God, and that he read to the Assembly the words of the gospel, outside of which peace is but an illusion.

Philippe Mottu has reported what one member of our government stated: " Switzerland's policy can only be one of love."

Thus the organic process of reconstructing the world, in conformity with both nature and revelation, goes through certain progressive stages: the restoration of the person, the personal vocation, the group vocation, and the national vocation.

Since the Renaissance there has been a problem that cannot be solved apart from God: the problem of the individual's relationship to the community. If, as contemporary Western culture has had it, the individual makes himself the primary reality and demands his independence and wishes to see in society nothing but a collection of individuals, he will fall into confusion, aloneness, and fear, the very state that begets unending conflict and discontent.

If the state makes itself the primary reality and sees the individual as only a tool in its power, then it will destroy the very source of all spiritual life, the human soul. It will become a religion, a tower of Babel destined to fall and disperse. " The individual is defined in relation to the state," wrote Gonzague de Reynold, " whereas the person is defined in relation to God."

Seen in the calmness of historical philosophy, Marxism, communism, nazism and fascism have been instructive attempts at answering the tremendous longing, which modern individualism has engendered, for a co-operative society. What gave Marxism its temporary popularity was that it gave the worker the " mystique " he felt need of in order to be part of a messianic cause that was far greater than himself. The thing that attracted so many people to the French Revolution, with its Freemasonry and its totalitarianism, was that they found in it the brotherhood that was no longer to be found in the church.

None of these attempts has really solved the social problem. It remains for us to tackle. Here in our country we need to undertake this task in practical fashion in order to be of help to the other nations of the world.

Many of our leaders clearly sense this today. Federal councilor Kobelt said: " Unlimited individual freedom obstructs the creation and development of a truly national community based on justice. Unlimited power of the state over the individual paralyzes the living and creative impulses of the personality, saps initiative, and impedes the development of the nation. Neither unrestricted freedom for business and industry, nor their complete control, can constitute the basis for a new Swiss economic order. . . . It is not a matter of subjugating the individual to the mass, but of incorporating him into the fellowship of free citizens. . . . Yet, voluntary incorporation presupposes a change in our way of thinking. It demands that we recognize that only a strong community can provide the foundation of security, of cultural development, and of well-being for the individual. On the other hand it requires us to see that only strong personalities, ready to shoulder responsibility, can form an enduring community."

This " change in our way of thinking" amounts to conversion. Thus on every hand we hear talk of a " return to spiritual values." We rejoice in this, but we have seen too many human ideologies go astray and fall apart, and we remember Gonzague de Reynold's remark, " There are no spiritual values apart from Christianity." Precisely because Christianity is not limited to a change in our way of thinking, it brings about a change of heart as well. Without this, the most largehearted ideas will end up only in renewed hostilities.

Bishop Marius Besson has put it well: " Switzerland will be Christian to the extent that its children will be Christian." What everyone of us can do, both for our country and for the world, is to dedicate our lives to Jesus Christ.

Certain experiments made during these last few years of war economy have proved most hopeful. Men, because they experienced an inner conversion in these experiments, have begun to develop a system of social thought and action far more promising that the most imperious demands for change.

A few years ago some intellectuals from France and Switzerland felt the need of our time and constituted themselves into the Community of Cluny. Their hope was quite secular — simply to escape their isolation. Soon they discovered that " apart from unity in Christ there can be no fellowship, but only association." Each passed through a spiritual self-consecration. In a strong discipline of common worship they developed the solid basis of their community. There is no other way.

Only the spirit of Christ can free men from their natural tendencies, which we have studied in order. Only his spirit can free them from formalism, independence, greed, and resentment, which stand in the way of the spirit of fellowship.

BIBLIOGRAPHICAL REFERENCES

Beaudoin, Ch., *La force en nous*. Editions du Mont-Blanc, Geneva and Annemasse, 1942.

Berdiaeff, Nicolas, *Destination de l'homme*. Payot, Paris.

Bergson, Henri, *Les deux sources de la morale et de la religion*. 1932.

Biot, R., *Le corps et l'âme*. Plon, Paris.

Biran, Maine de, *Journal intime*. Editions de La Vallette-Monbrun, Paris.

Bovet, Lucien, *De l'angoisse*. Payot, Lausanne, 1943.

Bovet, Théo, *Crédo Helvétique*. Delachaux et Niestlé, Neuchâtel, 1942.

Burnier, Edouard, *Révélation chrétienne et jugement de valeur religieux*. F. Roth, Lausanne, 1942.

Dalbiez, Roland, *La méthode psychanalytique et la doctrine freudienne*. Desclée et Brouwer, Paris, 1936.

Dubois, *Les psychonévroses et leur traitement moral*. Masson, Paris, 1905.

Ducommun, C. F., *La Suisse forge son destin*. Editons Labaconnière, Neuchâtel.

Ducommun, C. F., and Mottu, Philippe, *Pierres d'angle de la reconstruction nationale*. Delachaux et Niestlé, Neuchâtel et Paris, 1941.

Duhamel, Georges, "De la circulation par consentement mutuel," *Gazette de Lausanne*, 12 octobre, 1943.

Durand-Pallot, Ch., *Combien d'enfants?* J. H. Jeheber, Geneva, 1939.

Foot, Stephen, *Ma vie a commencé hier*. Payot, Lausanne, 1935.

Forel, O., "Psychologie de l'insécurité: Peur, panique, et politique," *Revue suisse de psychologie*, Nos. 1 and 2, 1942.

Gotthelf, Jeremias, *Geld und Geist*.

Huguenin, Elisabeth, *La femme devant son destin*. Editions Labaconnière, Neuchâtel, 1942.

—— *Mission de la femme.* Editions Labaconnière, Neuchâtel, 1940.

Jones, E. Stanley, *Vie victorieuse,* tr. from English by E. Leprieur. J. H. Jeheber, Geneva.

Jung, C. G., *Etudes de psychanalyse.*

Keller, Tina, *L'âme et les nerfs.* Payot, Lausanne, 1940.

Lecomte du Noüy, *L'avenir de l'Esprit.* Gallimard, Paris, 1941.

—— *Le temps et la vie.* Gallimard, Paris, 1936.

Lemoine, G., " Pourquoi le pain est-il mauvais? " *L'information médicale,* 1 juillet, 1938.

Liengme, G., *Pour apprendre à mieux vivre: Conseils pratiques aux nerveux.* V. Attinger, Neuchâtel, 1936.

Loebel, J., *Ayons confiance dans la médecine.* Plon, Paris, 1935.

Méautis, G., *Nicolas de Flue.* Editions Labaconnière, Neuchâtel, 1940.

Missenard, André, *A la recherche du temps et du rythme,* préface du Dr. A. Carrel. Plon, Paris, 1940.

Munthe, Axel, *Le livre de San Michele.* Albin Michel, Paris.

Olivier, E., *Médecine et santé dans le pays de Vaud au 18ᵉ siècle.*

Pascal, *Pensées.*

Plato, *Le banquet.*

Plutarch, *Des délais de la justice divine.* Amitiés gréco-suisses, Lausanne, 1935.

Raymond, Rev. Fr. V., O. P., *Le guide des nerveux et des scrupuleux.* Beauchesne, Paris, 1926.

Rougemont, Denis de, *Mission ou démission de la Suisse.* Editions Labaconnière, Neuchâtel, 1940.

—— *Penser avec les mains.* Albin Michel, Paris, 1936.

Rousseau, J. J., *Le contrat social.*

Sabatier, Paul, *Vie de St. François d'Assise.* Fischbacher, Paris, 1931.

Sertillanges, A. D., R. P., *La vie intellectuelle.* Editions de la Revue des Jeunes, Paris, 1921.

Thibon, Gustave, *Diagnostics.* Librairie de Médicis, Paris, 1940.

Thooris, A., *La médecine morphologique.* Doin, Paris, 1937.

Vincent, *Vers une médecine humaine*. Aubier, Collection "Esprit," Paris.

Weatherhead, L. D., *Psychologie, religion et guérison*, tr. from English by Amy Borgeaud. J. H. Jeheber, Geneva.

Weidle, Wladimir, *L'homme et le péché*. Plon, Paris, 1938.

Zuckermann, S., *La vie sexuelle et sociale des singes*, tr. from German by A. Petitjean. Gallimard, Paris.